Information Rights
in Practice

The non-legal professional's guide

Alan Stead

facet publishing

Published by Facet Publishing,
7 Ridgmount Street, London WC1E 7AE
www.facetpublishing.co.uk

Facet Publishing is wholly owned by CILIP: the Chartered Institute
of Library and Information Professionals.

British Library Cataloguing in Publication Data
A catalogue record for this book is available from the British Library.

ISBN 978-1-85604-620-6

First published 2008

Typeset from authors' files in 11/15 pt Bergamo
and Chantilly by Facet Publishing.
Printed and made in Great Britain by
MPG Books Ltd, Bodmin, Cornwall.

Contents

11   The public interest test 125

12   Publication schemes 131

13   Compliance, the Information Commissioner and the Information Tribunal 135

Acknowledgements

Thanks must go to Andy Gray of Ashfield District Council who spent many weekends checking the validity of the text, also to Susan Healey of The National Archives and Jim Wretham of OPSI for their time and assistance in preparing the chapters on Records Management and Re-use of Public Sector Information.

Finally without the support and assistance of my wife, Doreen, this book would not have got past the ideas stage. She has encouraged me to proceed when times were difficult and has also spent countless hours reading and checking over the book.

Disclaimer

The contents of this book are intended to raise awareness and suggest solutions. The book does not contain legal advice and should not be relied upon as such. While the advice and information contained in the book are believed to be true and accurate at the date of going to press, neither the author nor CILIP can accept any legal responsibility or liability for any errors or omissions that may be made.

Copyright

Table of statutes and case law

Acts of Parliament

Statutory Instruments

European Directives

Case Law

Tribunal and Information Commissioner Decision notices

Abbreviations

ACPO	Association of Chief Police Officers
ALMO	Arms length management authority
APPSI	Advisory Panel on Public Sector Information
ASB	Anti social behaviour
BAU	Business as usual
BSI	British Standards Institute
CCTV	Closed Circuit Television
CPS	Crown Prosecution service
CSA	Child Support Agency
DCA	Department for Constitutional Affairs (now Ministry of Justice)
DCLG	Department for Communities and Local Government
DEFRA	Department for Environment, Food and Rural Affairs
DHSS	Department for Health and Social Security (now Department of Health)
DPA	Data Protection Act 1998
DPP	Director of Public Prosecutions
DWP	Department for Work and Pensions
EDRM	Electronic Document and Records Management
EIR	Environmental Information Regulations 2004
FOI	Freedom of Information Act 2000
FPS	Fax Preference Service
FSA	Financial Services Authority

GIS	Geographical Information Systems
HMSO	Her Majesty's Stationery Office
ICC	Interception of Communications Commissioner
ICCO	Interception of Communications Commissioner's Office
ICO	Information Commissioner's Office
IFTS	Information Fair Trader Scheme
LLM	Law degree
MPS	Mail Preference Service
NAIM	National Association for Information Management
OPSI	Office of Public Sector Information
PSI	Re-use of Public Sector Information Regulations 2005
QC	Queen's Counsel
RIPA	Regulation of Investigatory Powers Act 2000
RSA	Rural Support Agency
Sch	Schedule
SCO	Surveillance Commissioner's Office
SI	Statutory Instrument
SPoC	Single Point of Contact
SRO	Senior Responsible Officer
TNA	The National Archives
TPS	Telephone Preference Service

1

Introduction

1.1   Overview

Information rights legislation has been described in the appeal courts as being amongst the most complex laws on the UK statute books; however, it does affect all of us in some way or another. There are those who want to access information about a public authority, or personal data held about themselves by organizations. They may be concerned about the way their personal data is being handled or may want to use data about someone else to process for themselves or to share with others; they may even just be in the street and be being filmed by the town's CCTV system. Everyone is affected by the way in which companies and public authorities handle information. The following chapters will guide you through the legislation in a clear, practical way, giving a greater understanding for both requesters and practitioners in this complex subject.

A growing number of people are now involved in the implementation of the legislation, particularly in the public sector. Information rights are rapidly becoming recognized as a profession and universities are starting to provide degree courses at both honours and master's levels.

It is actually a fascinating subject, giving professionals an insight into all aspects of the organization they work for. The Acts themselves are also open to interpretation, allowing the courts and the Information Tribunal to have a wider scope in the way the legislation is interpreted.

The dangers that hide beneath the pages of the legislation are the deadlines, which are themselves statutory, but which it is often outside the control of information rights staff to meet because other departments may have difficulty in supplying data on time.

This highlights the need, within public authorities especially, for a change in culture. Gone are be the days when authorities only told people what they wanted them to know.

Excuses heard for not releasing the information include, 'They have never had it before', 'What do they want that for?', 'What's it got to do with them?'

Problems are sometimes created by the Data Protection Act 1998 being wrongly applied for non release of information. Information rights does affect the whole of the authority and, without full commitment, can eventually result in major embarrassing or even legal consequences. Towards the end of 2006 Liverpool City Council was taken to court for non compliance and received a small fine of £350. Training and awareness of all staff, especially those who make the decisions and those on the front line are essential to the operation of the authority. Information rights professionals may get pressure from top management not to release sensitive information. The Information Commissioner's Office has advised that in these cases the professionals should record their views and make sure those wanting to change their decision also write down the reasons for overruling. If there is an appeal to the Information Commissioner, then at least both views will be available for him to consider.

It is a case for concern when organizations have two, three or even four different departments covering information rights. Separate sections covering data protection, freedom of information, environmental information and records management will not work unless they all talk on a regular basis. There is even a requirement under the codes of practice for records management issued under section 46 of the Freedom of Information Act 2000, for records management to be included alongside the information rights manager. A request can easily come under at least two and occasionally three different enactments and is a lot easier to handle if all are dealt with under the one department. The following is an example of a simple request which covers three different areas:

Dear Sir

I am concerned that you are thinking of closing Umbridgeshire Infant School. What is the decision making process behind this and where will my son be placed?

Can I also have my son's school records as I believe a move will affect him and I want to see where he is now?

Yours faithfully

Jane Brown

As you will see when you go further into the chapters, this actually covers three pieces of legislation, the Data Protection Act 1998, the Freedom of Information Act 2000 and the Data Protection Education Regulations, which it would be very difficult to collate if the function were not coordinated in one place.

In this book the chapters are organized by the various pieces of legislation for ease of reference, but do not be surprised if, when reading about, say, 'definition of personal data' you come across references to the Freedom of Information Act 2000 and the Environmental Information Regulations 2004, as to separate them is almost impossible.

1.2   History

Information rights is the overarching heading for everything under the Data Protection Act 1998, the Freedom of Information Act 2000, the Environmental Information Regulations 2004 and the Public Sector Information Regulations 2005.

Data protection started life under the Data Protection Act 1984 which related only to electronically held information and was controlled by the Data Protection Registrar. There was, at this stage, no European pressure to apply the legislation. The Act gave the Registrar very little actual power other than to criticize the authority breaching the Act. Registration was also difficult, as each application was registered separately and it was necessary for individuals who wanted to access their own data to write to the data controller of the authority concerned specifying under which registration their data was held and, if the information they wanted spread across a number of registrations, a separate fee was requested for each one. It is no wonder that the number of requests were few and far between.

It was not until 1995 that the European Parliament issued a directive, (EC) 95/46, which strengthened the protection of personal data across Europe. Most European countries welcomed this and created new legislation; only one or two felt their own Acts were strong enough to meet the new requirements, although even these are now amending them. Fortunately the United Kingdom decided that its own legislation needed rewriting and the then Lord Chancellor's Department introduced the Data Protection Act 1998.

The Data Protection Act 1998 is unique in information rights legislation in two ways. Firstly it not only tells how to access data but also how to handle and process it, and secondly it applies to all organizations, not just the public sector.

The Environmental Information Regulations 2004 also has its history in Europe. In 1992 the first Environmental Information Regulations were created in response to the European Directive (EC) 313/90. It is unclear how frequently this was invoked by public authorities but it was certainly not as widely proclaimed as the new regulations.

The conference on climate change at Kyoto in 1997 and the Aarhus Convention on Access to Information in 2001 both encouraged freer access to environmental data and this was endorsed at the Johannesburg World Summit on Sustainable Development in August 2002.

As a result of this increased awareness worldwide, the European Community, as a signatory to the Aarhus Convention, created a new directive, (EC) 2003/4, on which the UK Environmental Information Regulations 2004, which was passed on 10 December 2004, is based. This is actually a statutory instrument and not primary law but comes under the Act which enables European law to become national statute (European Communities Act 1972, Section 2(2)).

Freedom of information has also been around for a long time in Europe although it is unique among information rights legislation in that it is not based on European law. The United Kingdom seems to have come along on the third wave of legislation. Sweden started things rolling in the 18th century; more recently countries such as Australia, Canada, the United States of America and the Republic of Ireland brought in their legislation. Following the United Kingdom's example, other European countries such as France and Germany are watching with interest. The United Kingdom studied those that had gone before and saw a variety of approaches. Some will only accept requests from within their own country (Canada). Others insist that the request must show which legislation is applicable (Republic of Ireland). Some have a prohibitive charging scheme, such as that in the Republic of Ireland where a standard fee plus copying and postage costs for the request (around €15 is payable), a larger fee for a complaint (around €75) and over €100 for a complaint to the Commissioner. They report a drop in requests since this charging scheme was introduced. Other countries only allow a very short time to find and supply the data, around seven days in Estonia.

The Department for Constitutional Affairs, now the Ministry of Justice, report that the United Kingdom's laws are among the most accessible in the world and their introduction throughout the United Kingdom is being watched with interest by countries considering their own access to information legislation.

1.3   Summary

Information rights can be the most interesting job around. It enables practitioners to have an insight into their own authority and it is continually developing, with not only new legislation but new interpretations. The Data Protection Act has a number of case law examples whereas the other enactments are still relying on the decisions of the Information Commissioner. There are now a few Information Tribunal decisions, which can also help.

If it is a matter of interpretation, one view is as good as another, providing all the relevant issues have been taken into account and, it is suggested, have been documented. So, welcome to the fascinating world of information rights.

The next chapter introduces the Data Protection Act 1998, this being the oldest of the main information rights trilogy.

2

Data Protection Act 1998

2.1 Introduction

'Probably one of the most complex enactments on the statute book', says a judge in the UK Court of Appeal. As you have already seen this Act has evolved from European Directive (EC) 95/46, so the ultimate point of appeal is to the European Courts. It is primary legislation which has a big impact on all of our lives regardless of where we work.

The danger comes when individuals either disregard the Act completely or apply it where it should not be applied. It is not here to stop people working or sharing data, but to protect personal data and allow access to most of that which is held by authorities or companies.

Some high-profile cases in the courts have raised awareness of the Act and indicated where it can protect data and even where it cannot. Cases that are of interest include *Douglas and others* v. *Hello! Ltd* [2003]. Here photographs were taken of a celebrity wedding which were claimed to be in breach of the Act. This was an interesting case as it was argued that privacy had not been breached because another magazine was already taking photographs of the wedding with a view to publishing them. Another was the matter of *Regina* v. *Huntley* [2005], better known as the Soham murders, where a police force wrongly claimed that data on the defendant could not be shared under the Data Protection Act 1998 and there was a lack of a clear retention policy for documents. This case was followed by an in-depth study of the way that the Huntley information was handled, and resulted in revised procedures for handling data in the public sector (Bichard Inquiry, 2004).

The government is concerned that the Act is getting a bad name. It could be very easy for individuals to hide behind the legislation and claim that they do not want to release information because they cannot do so under the Data Protection Act. It should be remembered that the Act only covers personal data – as it is defined in Chapter 3, and that its purpose is not to inhibit data sharing – and that it can not only help to protect an individual's data but also help data sharing by ensuring all the necessary safeguards are in place, making the data reliable in a court of law.

When working with the Act the main things to always be considered are the eight data protection principles which are explained at Chapter 5 and the scope of the Act, covered in Chapter 4. With these in mind an organization will not go far wrong. None of the information rights legislation stands in isolation from other laws and reference should always be made to these other enactments when looking at the Act. This is particularly important when data sharing, as will be seen in Chapter 7, where some of these other enactments will be highlighted. Similarly, when dealing with requests for personal data it is possible that access to what is perceived to be personal data may also be covered by other legislation, as was seen in Chapter 1.

2.2   Definitions

Like most Acts, or even in most professions, there are words and phrases which have specific meanings. This is particularly relevant to data protection and before looking at the Act's requirements it would be useful to establish some of these.

2.2.1   Data controller

A data controller means

> a person who (either alone or jointly or in common with other persons)
> determines the purposes for which and the manner in which any personal data
> are, or are to be, processed.   (DPA 1998, s. 1(1))

It is the organization that processes data which is the data controller and not an individual, so this covers the whole of an organization. There are exceptions to this if parts of the organization are created by separate statute. For example, a local government authority covers all of the authority except the Registrar's office (births marriages and deaths), HM Coroner, Elections, the Youth Offending team, individual schools and two-thirds of an elected councillor's duties. One-third of the councillor's work is covered when they are doing work as required of them by a board, committee or panel.

2.2.2   Data processor

Section 1 of the Act describes a data processor:

> in relation to personal data, means any person (other than an employee of the data controller) who processes the data on behalf of the data controller.
>
> (DPA 1998, s. 1(1))

This would suggest that there is some form of contract between two parties to carry out work on behalf of an organization. The data controller is still responsible for the contractor's work and the contractor only acts as though they are the data controller's employee. There is not a need for the contractor to register with the Information Commissioner their intention to process data on the data controller's behalf (see Chapter 4.8). The data processor cannot, however, use the data for their own purposes.

2.2.3   Data subject

Quite simply a data subject is

> an individual who is the subject of the data.   (DPA 1998, s. 1(1))

This is the person who is the main purpose of the data request or sharing. The actual definition of personal data relating to a data subject is examined in more detail in Chapter 3.

2.2.4   Processing

The Act defines processing as

> in relation to information or data, means obtaining, recording or holding the information or data or carrying out any operation or set of operations on the information or data. Including
> (a) organisation, adaptation or alteration of the information or data,
> (b) retrieval, consultation or use of the information or data,
> (c) disclosure of the information or data by transmission, dissemination, or otherwise making available, or
> (d) alignment, combination, blocking erasure or destruction of the information or data.
>
> (DPA 1998, s. 1(1))

This suggests that the data controller will have to do something to the data in order for 'processing' to apply. The list in the Act is not, however, exhaustive, the word 'including' is used, so there may be other things that can be done to the data which will bring it under the heading of 'processing'. Court decisions have indicated, however, that the fact of transferring data from one place to another is not processing. It is only when something is actually done to the data that processing takes place. In the case of Johnson Medical Defence Union [2006] the court stated that the fact of moving data from one record to another to collate the information for subsequent analysis did not constitute 'processing'.

2.2.5   Relevant filing system

The definition of personal data given in the Act at section 1:

> Means any set of information relating to individuals to the extent that, although the information is not processed by means of equipment operating automatically in response to instructions given for that purpose

i.e. a computer

the set is structured, either by reference to individuals or by reference to criteria relating to individuals, in such a way that specific information relating to a particular individual is readily accessible.   (DPA 1998, s. 1(1))

The case of *Michael John Durant* v. *Financial Services Authority* [2003] has brought a great deal of dispute as to this ruling. In the Durant case the Court decided, although it was not the issue in question in the case, that a relevant filing system did not mean that a file simply had to have a name on it but that the content of the file should be referenced in such a way as to make it readily accessible to the point where it was as easy to access as if it had been in electronic format. So a file arranged into general data such as date of birth, parents and siblings, and then correspondence, assessments, reports was all right as it was readily accessible but a file arranged in date order did not give ready access to the information needed. This decision was taken through the Appeal Court to the House of Lords and may be disputed in the European Court.

Then along came the Freedom of Information Act 2000 which looked at the rights of access to unstructured data held by public authorities. Two additional sections were added to the Data Protection Act by the Freedom of Information Act (sections 68 to 73). The first was to add section 9A to the Data Protection Act. This section is worded in a somewhat complicated manner but actually defines unstructured data as

not being structured data

and goes on to state that a request must also describe the data. This is to help locate the data, so a general 'I want everything' request is not good enough.

It also, at subsection 3 of section 9A, applies the appropriate limit of work, currently £600 for central government (and Scotland) and £450 for non central government, calculated at £25 an hour, before any fee can be charged and then the fee is the same as under the Freedom of Information Act. Therefore for the public sector only, unstructured data is still accessible, but the Freedom of Information rules for charging will apply.

The Freedom of Information Act also adds section 33A to the Data Protection Act. This states that data under paragraph (e) of the definition of data under section 1(1) are exempt from principles one, two, three, five, seven and eight. These are

> fairly and lawfully processed,
> can only be used for one or more specified purposes,
> must be adequate, relevant and not excessive,
> must be not kept longer than necessary,
> must be secure,

and

> not be transferred outside EEA.

Paragraph (e) was amended under section 68 of the Freedom of Information Act to include any information held by a public authority not included in the other definitions. This type of data is also exempt from section 55,

> unlawful use of data.

More of this later in Chapter 13, Compliance.

Section 70(2) of the Freedom of Information Act is more helpful as it adds that personal data of an employee of the Crown or public authority not held in a structured filing system are exempt from the remaining data protection principles.

2.3   Summary

The Data Protection Act should always be seen as an opportunity to share or provide data, not a deterrent. As you have seen, it can affect both working and private lives and it is always worth considering that while you may be looking at this legislation from the point of view of an organization, the rights attributed to an individual also apply to others of the same organization. Before the Act is examined in detail it will be useful to know what is meant by 'personal data'.

3

Definitions of personal data

3.1   Introduction

The Data Protection Act 1998 only applies to living individuals and describes two different types of personal data. The first relates to most of the data held about individuals and the second to sensitive personal data which it then goes on to define. The first test of data is always, 'Is it personal?', and only if this condition is met can the sensitive data test be applied.

Personal data can be held, as will be seen in Chapter 5, without specific consent of the subject so long as they are aware that the data is being held and why. Sensitive data can only be held with specific consent and this will be examined later in this chapter.

The definition of personal data is vital to the operation not only of this Act but also of the other main legislation in the information rights set. These remaining enactments both have sections which exempt personal data from their provisions. In the Freedom of Information Act 2000 this is section 40 and in the Environmental Information Regulations 2004 it is regulation 13.

The Act itself leaves this area open to some interpretation. Section 1(1) describes personal data as follows:

'Personal data' means data which relate to a living individual who can be identified

(a) from those data, or

(b) from those data and other information which is in the possession of, or is
likely to come into the possession of, the data controller,

and includes any expression of opinion about an individual and any indication of
the intentions of the data controller or any other person in respect of the
individual.   (DPA 1998, s. 1(1))

3.2   Deceased persons

Firstly the Act only applies to living individuals. Data of persons who are
deceased no longer come under the Act although there are other laws
which relate to this type of data. Examples of some of these are: Access to
Health Records Act 1990 (this relates to access by the next of kin to health
records of the deceased), Local Government Finance Act 1992 (as it
relates to council tax data), and Human Rights Act 1998, Article 8 of
Schedule 1 (this article, lifted from the European directive, gives everyone
the right to respect for his private and family life, his home and his
correspondence). These particular rights extend after death and it is worth
considering any possible damage to the reputation of the deceased or their
family and friends before releasing information. Would the data be
released if the subject were alive? If so, then it probably should be released,
if not, then it should not. It should be noted from this that the rights of
other people such as relatives and their personal data still have to be taken
into account.

This particular area is important when reading through social services data
when an individual wishes to see their file (a right given under section 7 of
the Data Protection Act) with the purpose of finding out why they were
placed in care. It is necessary to consider carefully, if the birth parents are
deceased, what damage would be caused to other members of the family, to
the reputation of the deceased and, indeed, to the requester if the
information were not withheld.

3.3   Substantive personal data

The Act explains partly what is actually meant by personal data. You will recall that it includes any opinions or intentions about the individual as well as the basic facts about a person. It took a court case, however, to describe what were facts and what were not. In this case, *Michael John Durant v. FSA*. [2003], while it has caused some concern in its definition of relevant filing system, its definition of personal data is particularly helpful. Personal data has to tell us something substantive about an individual.

In this case the Financial Services Authority (FSA) had a file on a complaint made by Mr Durant. He was mentioned on the front cover but the information contained in the file told nothing about him, only about the complaint he had lodged. The Appeal Court decided that the file therefore contained no personal data. It further went on to state that personal data must tell more than just the name of an individual and must also tell something about that person.

3.4   Identified by secondary reference

You may have noticed that it is not only data such as a name that is regarded as personal, but also data which does not actually mention a name but from which a person can be identified as in the following example.

A reference to 'the Chief Executive of Umbridgeshire Council' clearly identifies an individual as there is only one person with this title. A reference to 'a clerk at Umbridgeshire Council' does not identify an individual and would therefore fall outside the Act. It would probably come under the Freedom of Information Act, however.

You have to look at the data controller and decide if that organization, or even an individual in that organization, could make a reference and identify an individual. If this is the case, then it would constitute personal data, as in the example below.

A payroll number of A1357 means very little and a report that the payee had received an overpayment would, for most people, not identify an individual. However the manager of A1357 would have access to that part of the payroll and would be able to identify the individual quite easily.

3.5 Third party data

In sections 7 and 8 of the Act there is reference to third party data. This is data which is not about the requester themselves but about someone else. This someone can be anyone who is not the subject and can include close relatives such as spouse, children and siblings.

There are certain requirements which have to be taken into account when dealing with data about third parties and they usually occur when a request has been made to view a file and it is found to contain data relating to another person. If that person is carrying out their official duties then they may be regarded as a relevant person, described below in section 3.6. This is also important if considering a request under the Freedom of Information Act, where the names of officials may not be regarded as personal data.

Therefore data about an individual other than the subject of the file is defined as third party and can only be accessed in accordance with sections 7 and 8 of the Act. These will be examined in more detail in Chapter 6.

3.6 Relevant persons

This leads us on to names of individuals carrying out duties connected to their employment. What does the fact that 'the Chief Executive, Mr Roberts, attended the opening of the new Library' tell us about Mr Roberts? Very little, in fact nothing personal about him at all other than the fact he is the Chief Executive, which is common knowledge. Similarly, requests for information, in the public sector, about the chief executive's salary and expenses could also not be regarded as personal information as they relate to him in a public capacity. This subject was discussed at length in an Information Commissioner's Decision Notice FS50062124 against Corby Borough Council, and in subsequent guidance on this subject issued by the Commissioner where the level of accountability and need to know how public funds are spent far outweighs any expectation of privacy for public officials.

Despite this argument, it may further be stated, however, that while the amount spent on a meal taken in the course of public duties should be disclosed, the actual type of meal may reveal something personal, such as religious beliefs or medical condition, and would be contrary to the requirements of sensitive data if it was released. Sensitive personal data will be defined later in this chapter. It will be seen that requests under both the Freedom of Information Act 2000 and the Environmental Information Regulations 2004 for what on the face of it might be regarded as personal data have to be handled on a case-by-case basis and that section 40 or regulation 13 exemptions or exceptions (both relate to personal data) might not apply, in fact in these instances would rarely do so.

The Data Protection Act defines these relevant persons under section 38 and its subsequent orders. These orders, SI 2000/413 (Health), SI 2000/414 (Education) and SI 2000/415 (Social Work), refer to accessible records and describe the professionals engaged in these areas as being relevant persons under the Act. This means that if their names occur within a social services or housing file they should be released to a requester unless it would cause damage or distress to the individual.

An example of how damage might be caused is given below. This is an actual case, although names have been changed.

Mr Telmark asked the local housing authority under section 7 of the Data Protection Act if he could have copies of his housing records. In his letter he voluntarily stated he was currently an inmate at Her Majesty's Prisons, where he had been sent for drug trafficking offences. He further described his purpose for requiring the files as being to identify the housing officer who had reported him to the police for suspected trafficking so he could speak to her. He paid his statutory fee of £10. The housing authority considered the request and was aware that the housing officer was a relevant person under the legislation but that in this case there was a strong possibility that she might be caused considerable damage or distress if her name were released, and redacted all reference to her from the file before sending it on to Mr Telmark.

It is strongly recommended that if a similar case occurs then a record of the decision-making process is kept, as it may not be quite as obvious as in this case. One test of this type of data is to examine the expected right of privacy of the individual. The higher up the tree a person is, or the stronger their accountability, then the lesser the expectation of privacy.

3.7   Sensitive personal data

The Act describes in Schedule 1 that

> in the case of sensitive personal data, at least one of the conditions in Schedule 3 is met.   (DPA 1998, Principle 1, Schedule 1)

These conditions are listed in Chapter 5, but note that to comply with this requirement it is necessary to know what is meant by 'sensitive data'. Fortunately section 2 of the Act gives an exhaustive list of what is regarded as sensitive.

> 2 In this Act 'sensitive personal data' means personal data consisting of information as to –
> (a) the racial or ethnic origin of the data subject,
> (b) his political opinions,
> (c) his religious beliefs or other beliefs of a similar nature,
> (d) whether he is a member of a trade union,
> (e) his physical or mental health or condition,
> (f) his sexual life,
> (g) the commission or alleged commission by him of any offence, or
> (h) any proceedings for any offence committed or alleged to have been committed by him, the disposal of such proceedings or the sentence of any court in such proceedings.
>
> (DPA 1998, s. 2)

This does not mean that the data cannot be processed but that to do so there is a need to comply with the various requirements of the Act. Most of these are listed in Schedule 3 of the Act and are explained later in

Chapter 5. It should be noted that this list is exhaustive and, although there may be other issues you feel should be added (such as age), or even removed, these are not currently sensitive.

This list is all-encompassing so, for example, it is of no matter how minor an illness is, it is all regarded as sensitive. It is understood that there may be statutory requirements to process this data and these issues are also covered under Schedule 3 of the Act.

3.8   Summary

Like most of the definitions and interpretations in all the information rights legislation, decisions cannot be taken to cover whole groups of data but must be applied on a case-by-case basis. However, the specific legislation applied has a major impact on the definition used and what information can be released, particularly if this is to a third party. More difficulty can be experienced when looking at data which does not include a name, such as in the earlier case of the chief executive, or other information which could tell you about an individual. More guidance in this area will be provided in Chapter 6.

Now that you are aware of what is regarded as personal data we will look at the scope of the legislation, which, you will find, extends outside the area of pure access.

4

The scope of the Data Protection Act

4.1 Introduction

The UK Data Protection Act 1998's main functions are connected with access to data. However, there are other parts of the Act that need to be considered and these will be looked at in this chapter. Some of the issues examined will relate to definitions that have not already been mentioned in Chapters 2 and 3. Other topics will include parts of the Act which do not fit happily into any of the other chapters.

4.2 Credit reference agencies

It is assumed that a request made to a credit reference agency for data relates to the requester's financial standing. The request is made under section 7 of the Act, which relates to making a request and will be mentioned in Chapter 6. However, it is also covered by section 9 of the Act, which relates solely to these agencies, as other legislation such as section 159 of the Consumer Credit Act 1974 also has an effect on them. Do not forget that the timescale is different for supplying the data – seven days – and so is the fee, currently £2.50 (Data Protection (fees under section 19/7) Regulations 2000).

4.3   Right to stop processing

There are a number of issues under section 10 of the Act relating to processing. Firstly the requester can give notice that the data controller must

> cease or not to begin, processing . . . any personal data in respect of which he is a data subject.   (DPA 1998, s. 10(1))

Of course it would be necessary to prove that there was a likelihood of damage or distress and that the processing was not warranted. So using their data to arrest an individual would cause them distress, but would be warranted. The data controller must reply within 21 days to tell the requester that they have complied or why they will not comply. A court can force a data controller to comply if it agrees with the requester.

4.4   Compensation – damage and distress

Compensation is very difficult to obtain under the Act. A person can get compensation for damage or damage and distress but not for distress on its own. The person must prove some actual damage, a brick through the window for example (section 13).

The first illustration shows how embarrassment has been caused, but not actual damage.

A gentleman bought a property in a particular town. A few years later he sold the property and moved out of the area. He informed his local authority that he had done this and that he was no longer liable for council tax. The council did not amend the records and sent him further demands for tax, even threatening to send a bailiff. This letter was opened by the new owners; the name had slipped up in the window of the envelope. The gentleman complained and the council apologized and wrote to him and the current owners admitting the mistake. The Information Commissioner stated that the council had rectified the error and so no further action was necessary and although the gentleman had been embarrassed this did not constitute damage.

The second illustration shows how easy it is to let something slip and allow actual damage to occur.

A complaint was received regarding misuse of a property and the public authority interviewed the tenant, who had a friend with him. There was no case to answer so the officer in charge of the investigation told the complainant this. The complainant then stated that a Mr X should be consulted. Mr X was in fact the friend of the tenant and had already been interviewed and this information was passed on to the complainant. Mr X had a brick through his window that night and received verbal abuse from the local inhabitants when he went out.

In this case Mr X had actually suffered physical damage and a claim could be made.

4.5   Direct marketing

We have all been subject to those annoying phone calls in the middle of dinner stating that Double Glazed Windows Ltd (a fictitious company) will be in the area next week and you are one of the chosen few. At last you can stop this without having to write to every double glazing company in the country stating that they must not send this information to you. If you put your address, telephone (including mobile) or fax number on the appropriate preference list then, after 28 days, the notice to cease must apply. This prohibition relates to the telephone number or address, not to the person, so if you change address you must reapply, although the notice applies until reversed by the subscriber. However, make sure that you haven't given permission for cold calling when filling in forms. You should be given the option to say your contact data must not be used for direct marketing. If you do let one slip by you can always cancel it at any time.

If you do not want your information to be used for marketing, do not give it out unless there is a real need. This will be mentioned again later under the data protection principles in Chapter 5.

The contact details for the preference services are:

Mailing Preference Service (MPS) Freepost 22

London W1E 7EZ   020 7766 4410

Telephone Preference Service (TPS)   0845 070 0707

Fax Preference Service (FPS)   0845 070 0702

E-mail Preference Service (only works if the message

comes from inside Europe)   www.e-mps.org/en

This ruling also applies, since 2004, to business addresses and phone numbers and even to direct dial numbers. The ruling is called The Privacy and Electronic Communications (EC Directive) (amendment) Regulations 2004: SI 2004/1039. The registration does need to be renewed annually, however, in case there is a change of staff.

Now for the other side of the coin, where an organization may wish to carry out direct marketing. Some areas are obvious, where an organization wants to promote a course or facility it is running. Others are not so clear and the following example may clarify the situation where confusion can arise.

A human resources officer discovered that there were some staff who had their own pension schemes and did not contribute to the authority's scheme. The HR officer wanted to contact these people, at their home addresses, to point out the error of their ways and how they should consider changing to the scheme run by the authority. 'But it isn't marketing,' he claimed, 'it is for the benefit of the staff.' To which the answer came back from the information rights office, 'So is double glazing!'

It was suggested that the HR officer write to all staff at work, as this was not individually directed, if he wanted to get the message over.

Organizations should always look for an alternative that makes the marketing not directed to an individual – for example, by sending it to everyone without names or getting another department to send it out with its own forms. All this is covered by section 11 of the Act.

4.6   Automated processing

This is where data is fed into a computer and then it produces a decision without any human intervention, and reveals, for example, whether Mr Z can have a house or Miss V has a place on the course.

An individual can issue a notice under section 12 of the Act stating that the data controller cannot process any information which significantly affects them automatically This includes evaluating creditworthiness, reliability, conduct or work performance.

The data controller has 21 days in which to respond. He must also tell people if a decision has been made automatically and the individual has 21 days to instruct that the decision be made using manual methods if they believe it is being processed wrongly.

It should be remembered that if an individual asks for their personal data under section 7 of the Act and some of this was automatically processed they must be told how it was calculated in terms that are easily comprehended.

4.7   Rectification, blocking, erasure and destruction

Under section 14 of the Act an individual who can satisfy a court that the information held is inaccurate can ask the court to order that the information be changed, not used for processing, deleted or destroyed. Under this section the power to make the order lies with the court, so the individual cannot just write and force the data controller to change the data. However, the source of the information is irrelevant, so it could have come from the person themselves or from a third party. It would be usual for the court to direct that the incorrect data be replaced by new and accurate data and that anyone else to whom the data had been passed also be told of the changes.

4.8   Notification

As was already mentioned in Chapter 2, under the 1984 Data Protection Act life was quite simple; those processing data had to tell the data protection registrar if they did any processing electronically and had to register each application separately. This made data requests almost impossible for the applicant because they had to know not only who processed the data but also where it was processed. No wonder there were not that many data requests before 2000.

The 1998 Act put an end to that. With certain exceptions, any data controller must annually notify to the Information Commissioner the information as described at section 16:

(a) his name and address,

(b) if he has nominated a representative for the purposes of this Act, the name and address of the representative,

(c) a description of the personal data being or to be processed by or on behalf of the data controller and of the category or categories of data subject to which they relate,

(d) a description of the purpose or purposes for which the data are being or are to be processed,

(e) a description of any recipient or recipients to whom the data controller intends or may wish to disclose the data,

(f) the names or a description of any countries or territories outside the European Economic Area to which the data controller directly or indirectly transfers or intends or may wish directly or indirectly to transfer data, and

(g) in any case where data which is not covered by the notifications is processed, a statement to that fact.

(DPA 1998, s. 16(1))

Sections 16 to 20 explain how notification should be carried out and state that the Information Commissioner shall keep a public register of these notifications. This is online for inspection on the Commissioner's website (www.ico.gov.uk).

To make life easier, the Information Commissioner has provided some templates, so all that data controllers need to do is select the appropriate one, make any changes they feel are necessary and submit it annually to the Commissioner. He also reminds them each year when they must renew. For this there is a statutory annual fee of £35 and it takes about ten minutes online to do it. There has been a spate of rogue companies offering to do this task for data controllers. Some actually did the notification but many just pocketed the money and ran, or at best sent the same forms that the Commissioner would supply for free. Trading Standards and the Information Commissioner seem to have stopped most of these, but data controllers should be cautious.

Section 21 states that it is an offence to process data not on the register, however, it is a defence if it can be shown that the data controller had done everything he could to notify (section 21(3)).

People who process data (this includes Christmas card lists), purely for accounting or personal use, or do not store their data electronically, need not register with the Commissioner, so a person who teaches, say, the piano, from home need not notify as long as the data is not used for advertising and the like; but it is always worth contacting the Information Commissioner's Office just to make sure. They are very helpful and will even complete some of the forms for you if you are having difficulties.

Under section 20 the data controller also has only 28 days to notify any changes to the register. However, this does not mean that a change from a manual to a computerized system needs to be re-registered. It is only if the process changes or includes a new purpose – like using CCTV for monitoring staff – and this has not been mentioned under the relevant element.

The notification is one way to inform individuals what is done with their data and also goes some way towards the data audit that needs to be carried out (see Chapter 15), as it should show all the personal data in an authority.

4.9   Summary

The rights that have been covered in this chapter constitute the main elements of the sixth data protection principle under Schedule 1 of the Act,

Personal data shall be processed in accordance with the rights of the data subjects under this Act.

The importance of these sections, in conjunction with the rights of access, which will be found in Chapter 6, are therefore of great importance to the understanding and implementation of the legislation.

This leads to the next chapter, examining the Act's eight principles.

5

The data protection principles

5.1   Introduction

The eight data protection principles form the backbone of the legislation and when discussing data protection issues it is often necessary to keep referring back to them and establishing the appropriate principle to apply. They are all listed in Schedule 1 to the Act but frequent reference to the main sections of the Act is needed for clarification. They are also shown in Appendix 1 of this book.

Section 4 of the Data Protection Act states that

> References in this Act to the data protection principles are to the principles set out in Part 1 of Schedule 1.

The principles as listed in the Schedule are:

1. Personal Data shall be processed fairly and lawfully and, in particular, shall not be processed unless:-
   a) at least one of the conditions at Schedule 2 is met, and
   b) in the case of sensitive data, at least one of the conditions at Schedule 3 is also met.
2. Personal data shall be obtained for one or more specified and lawful purposes, and shall not be further processed in a manner incompatible with that purpose or those purposes.

3. Personal data shall be adequate, relevant and not excessive in relation to the purpose or purposes for which they are provided.
4. Personal data shall be accurate and, where necessary, kept up to date.
5. Personal data processed for any purpose or purposes shall not be kept for longer than is necessary for that purpose or purposes.
6. Personal data shall be processed in accordance with the rights of the data subject.
7. Appropriate technical and organisational measures shall be taken against unauthorised or unlawful processing of personal data and against accidental loss or destruction, or damage to, personal data.
8. Personal data shall not be transferred to a country or territory outside the European Economic Area unless that country or territory ensures an adequate level of protection for the rights and freedoms of data subjects in relation to the processing of personal data.

(DPA 1998, Schedule 1)

It is possible that more than one principle may apply to any set of personal data and therefore the principles are not mutually exclusive. In this chapter we will look at each of these principles in some reasonable depth and see how they can be applied in practice.

5.2   The principles

5.2.1   Principle 1 – Processed fairly and lawfully

This is probably the most important of all the principles and receives a reasonable amount of guidance in Part II of Schedule 1 in the Act so it is best to approach it in segments.

Fair processing

A fair processing statement is required whenever data is collected. Individuals need to be told why the data is wanted, what will be done with it and to whom it will be passed (Schedule 1 Part II, paragraph 3 and section 7 (1)). This is shown in detail in Chapter 6. A simple comment at the bottom of a form, such as the following would be a sufficient fair processing statement.

'Your data is being collected for the purposes described on this form and will not be used for any other purpose or passed on to any other body, except as required by law, without your consent.'

This will, in most cases, suffice and if the intended use is for marketing the following can be added:

'Occasionally we may identify organizations that have services which may be of interest to you. If you (do not want us to) (would like us to) pass this information on to them please tick here.' Also of use is 'You may unsubscribe from this list at any time by contacting _____'

Part II of the Schedule requires that the purpose for which the data is being collected is made clear so that no one is misled. It also requires that the individual knows who is the data controller collecting the data.

Lawful processing

An individual can do anything they want as long as the law does not prohibit it. However, if you are part of a corporate body or public authority you can only do things the law permits. This is described in law as being *intra vires* (*intra* = within and *vires* = powers). The next question to ask is what law permits an organization to collect the data and keep a record of it. When another organization is asked to provide personal data it holds it should first check the legislation under which the data may be shared. As we shall see in Chapter 7, it is not the Data Protection Act that permits sharing, but another enactment relating to the purpose behind the sharing.

The principle goes on to say that in order to use personal data, then a condition of Schedule 2 or Schedule 3, if it is sensitive data (see Chapter 5 for the definition of personal and sensitive personal data), must be met. There are six Schedule 2 conditions, of which at least one must be met.

Schedule 2 conditions

- **The data subject gives consent to processing.**   (DPA 1998, Sch. 2(1))
  This is clear, but remember that consent can be withdrawn at any
  time and that the subject cannot give consent to an unlawful act.
  Therefore, if any enactment prohibits sharing, an individual cannot
  give consent to share. The secondary use of council tax data has
  always created a great deal of debate. The Local Government Finance
  Act (1992) states at Schedule 2, paragraph 17 that the Secretary of
  State can raise an order to permit the secondary use of council tax data
  unless it contains personal data, which, the schedule goes on to
  explain at paragraph 18, consists of a name (including that of a
  deceased person). The Secretary has not made any such order, but did
  amend the Schedule with the Local Government Act 2002 and the
  Housing Act 2004, which permits sharing, if it is to identify empty
  properties, by the collecting authority for their reuse. There is no
  other exemption from Schedule 2 in law. Therefore to reuse council
  tax data for another purpose would be contrary to the Local Government Finance Act 1992 and the Data Protection Act 1998, in that the
  processing is not lawful. Other than council tax, there are other Acts,
  such as the Enterprise Act 2002, which actually prohibit sharing.

- **Processing is necessary to perform a contract or, at the request of the subject,
  with a view to taking out a contract.**   (DPA 1998, Sch. 2(2))
  Remember that the other principles apply and the data collected
  must not be excessive and must be relevant. It could be argued that
  the fact that the subject has entered into a contract implies his
  consent to the processing.

- **Processing is necessary to carry out a legal obligation.**   (DPA 1998, Sch. 2(3))
  Again, it is necessary to find out what legal obligation is being
  imposed.

- **Processing is necessary to protect the vital interests of the subject.**
  (DPA 1998, Sch. 2(4))

This is defined by the Information Commissioner as a life-or-death situation. The purpose of the condition is to ensure that, in situations where the subject cannot reasonably give consent, his life is not put at risk by a reluctance to share essential information.

- Processing is necessary for the administration of justice, for the exercise of any functions conferred on any person by an enactment, of any functions of the Crown or Minister of the Crown or a government department, or of any other functions of a public nature exercised in the public interest by any person.

(DPA 1998, Sch. 2(5))

It is generally accepted that this condition covers only the person exercising the public function and not those gathering evidence to pass on, for example building a complaint to pass to an auditor. In this example the auditor would be covered by this condition as they would be carrying out the function, but the person making the initial complaint would not be.

- The sixth condition states that the data must be necessary for the legitimate interests pursued by the data controller, or third parties to whom the data is disclosed unless this will prejudice rights and freedoms or legitimate interests of the data subject. (DPA 1998, Sch. 2(6)(1)) This is not a catchall but allows organizations to collect information for their proper business. The condition therefore implies that if data is processed other than for the normal business of the organization this would be unlawful.

Schedule 3 conditions

Schedule 3 relates to sensitive data for which, as seen in Chapter 3, there has to be consent for processing. The difference from Schedule 2 conditions is that the Act actually states that

explicit consent is required.   (DPA 1998, Sch. 3(1))

in this section unless one of the conditions applies.

- The first of these conditions is

  The data subject has given his explicit consent to the processing.

  (DPA 1998, Sch. 3(1))

  Therefore just to tell the subject that the data will be held is not sufficient, he must also give consent.

- The schedule continues with

  Processing is necessary for the purposes of exercising or performing any right or obligation which is conferred or imposed by law on the data controller in connection with employment.   (DPA 1998, Sch. 3(2)(1))

  If there is a law which states that personal data shall be processed, then this overrides the conditions at Schedule 3. It should be considered, however, what the law is actually asking for and whether there are ways around the issue by giving non personal data. It is suggested that if statistical information would give the required answer, then sensitive personal information need not be released.

- The next point is

  Processing to protect the vital interests of the data subject or another person.

  (DPA 1998, Sch. 3(3)(a))

  This has a similar interpretation to paragraph 4 under Schedule 2, except this time it is explained better, stating that the exemption applies where consent cannot be given. The vital interest of another person, including in cases where consent has unreasonably been withheld, is also covered.

This could particularly apply to the NHS: 'Is there is a danger of contact with a contagious disease?'

As will be seen in Chapter 16, Schedule 3(3)(a) could be applied to override a person's right to privacy under Article 8 of the European Convention on Human Rights, and also under Schedule 1 of the Human Rights Act 1998. The vital interest of other persons overrides that of an individual's privacy – for example, in publishing the picture of a convicted murderer who has absconded from prison.

- Processing carried out in the course of its legitimate interest by any body or association.   (DPA 1998, Sch. 3(4)(a))

This is more restrictive, as the organization must be one that is not for profit or is for political, philosophical, religious or trade union purposes. It is further restrictive in that those whose data are being processed must be members of the organization or have regular contact with it. It does not give consent to share with a third party.

If the data subject has already made the information public, this is a good excuse for sharing it, as it is already in the public domain. Care must, however, be taken to establish when the information was made public. This is demonstrated in the following case before the European Court.

The case of *Peck v. United Kingdom* [2003]. This is a well-known case in which a man was identified on CCTV footage as attempting suicide. This image was later used by the media and he was easily identified by friends, which caused considerable distress. In this case Mr Peck complained through the media after the disclosure relating to him had already been made. The European Court judged that the fact that the press were aware after the event could not be used as a defence by the media and the authority for releasing the information in the first place.

- Data required

for or in conjunction with any legal proceedings, obtaining legal advice, or otherwise defending legal rights   (DPA 1998, Sch. 3(6))

is also permissible without consent. This has a similar meaning to section 35 of the Act, which will be looked at in Chapter 6.

- If data is required

for the administration of justice, any function conferred by an enactment or the function of the Crown, a Minister of the Crown or a government department
(DPA 1998, Sch. 3(7)(1))

this again is permissible. It should be noted that this only relates to actual government departments and not to agencies of government or other public sector authorities.

- Data required
  for medical purposes and is undertaken by health professionals
                                               (DPA 1998, Sch. 3(8)(1))
  can be shared. Note here the restriction of this exemption to
  medical use, providing that the data has been provided by health
  professionals or individuals with the same duty of care. If this is the
  case, then the data can be used without consent. This is also referred
  to in the final Schedule 3 condition.

- Equality laws state that monitoring of racial, ethnic, age or gender
  data must take place and concern is sometimes expressed about the
  collection of such data (Race Relations Act 1976). Paragraph 9,
  Schedule 3 of the Data Protection Act makes specific reference to
  this although it could be argued that it is also covered by paragraph
  7(b) of the Schedule,

  conferred by another enactment.

  However it does emphasize that appropriate safeguards have to be in
  place to look after the rights of the individual. There are a number
  of requirements, such as requests from government to monitor the
  ethnicity of staff, service users and so on. It is necessary to ask the
  purpose of the request and whether the requester needs to know
  names or is trying to establish a trend. The latter can easily be
  accomplished by statistics (e.g. 25% of applicants were from outside
  Europe). If names are requested, then the question has to be asked
  whether this is excessive (Data Protection Act Principle 3).

Provided that at least one of these conditions are met and that there is a
law that says sharing can take place, then Principle 1 can be met and
specific consent need not be obtained.

5.2.2   Principle 2 – Obtained for one or more purposes

Very simply, this means that data can only be used for the purpose for which it is collected. This is why the fair processing statement looked at earlier in this chapter has to be clear and cover everything that is required of the data. Also, the purpose must be listed in the organization's notification to the Information Commissioner. Chapter 4.8 explains this in more detail.

This is also particularly important when data is to be shared. It is clear from this that the location where data is shared is not as important as the purpose. The following scenario often occurs in large authorities.

It is frequently asked whether data can be shared and the argument is given, 'Well, we are the same authority'. This is irrelevant; data cannot be shared with the person in the next room if it is for a different purpose.

There are frequently ways around this, which are examined in Chapter 7.

5.2.3   Principle 3 – Adequate, relevant and not excessive

This is aimed at the 'wouldn't it be nice to have' scenario. It is also necessary to consider from how many people the information is needed, and if from only one, why it is being collected from everyone.

The example given below shows a common case which, applied to most organizations, could be regarded as being contrary to this principle.

A company used to collect the National Insurance number from all people who applied for jobs. This was because it was needed when they appointed the one successful applicant and it showed that they had a right to work in this country. The company was asked why, when applications would run to around 100 people for each job, they collected this information when it applied to only the one appointee. Now the company does not ask for this information on its application forms.

The information being collected should be looked at and the questions asked, 'Do I really need this? Can I manage without it? What has it got to do with the purpose?' If the answer is not positive to any of these, then the data should not be requested. Care should be taken in the designing of computer systems which require data to be entered, as this could also be against this principle (see the example given below under Principle 4).

5.2.4   Principle 4 – Accurate and kept up to date

The shortest of the principles, this nonetheless has a big impact on how the Act operates. Obviously the information can only be as accurate and up to date as that which is provided by the subject. However, it does put an obligation on data controllers to check periodically that the data has not changed.

The following is a common example of compliance with this principle.

Those with children at school will know that every year the school sends a form which shows, for example, that 'Johnny is now in year 6 and his teacher is Miss Murgatroid and he has sandwiches every Thursday etc.' This is the school complying with this principle.

Consider how frequently there is a likelihood of change and this will give an indication of how often it is necessary to check the data.

It is possible that an action may contravene more than one principle. The principles are not mutually exclusive and more than one may apply. The story below shows how this could happen.

A financial institution had a computer system that required date of birth to be entered. Not everyone gave the date of birth so staff would enter 01/01/00; therefore on the face of it they had some very young or very old applicants. When challenged, the manager was told that, if the information was necessary, they must check and get an accurate date of birth, as the one entered was not accurate. 'Not to worry', he said, 'we don't use the date of birth.' So why was it being collected? Remember Principle 3.

5.2.5 Principle 5 – Not kept for longer than is necessary

That is all the Act says and no further guidance is given. However, this is the main reference to records management in the Data Protection Act. This is brought out much more in the Freedom of Information Act 2000 under Section 46, where an entire code of practice has been issued, underlining the importance of this topic (see Chapter 15).

This is illustrated in the case of *Regina* v. *Huntley* (Soham murders) when there was criticism of a police force's retention schedules, or lack of them.

The National Archives refers to destruction schedules but the idea of retention helps to sell the idea more to the reluctant manager who has a loft mentality: 'I must keep this as it may come in useful one day.'

Records management is examined in more detail in Chapter 15, but at this point it is worth noting that data has a number of stages in its life. There is live data; then data which is not used but must be kept because there may be reference to it or because the law says it must be kept (this is retention data); and then it goes either to archive or destruction, depending on what it is. When data reaches the end of its prescribed retention period, it should be reviewed and then destroyed, archived if it has any historical value, or retained for a further short period if there is still a chance of its being referred to again.

The retention period should start when the records are no longer actively used. If they are still regularly required, then they should be kept active. This means that each case has to be taken on its own merits. The story below gives an example of how things can go wrong if this principle is not followed:

A financial institution was taking an individual to court for non payment of debt. It took a very long time to get to a hearing, some seven years, and the institution's own computer system automatically deleted records after six years. This meant that there was no evidence to produce to the court and the case fell.

Websites where examples of record retention periods for the various sections of the public sector can be found, and more details about records management, are in Chapter 15.

5.2.6   Principle 6 – Processed in accordance with the rights of the data subject

At this point it is necessary to hunt through the Act and find the rights that apply.

There is the right of access to personal data (section 7), right to prevent processing likely to cause damage or distress (section 10), right to prevent processing for direct marketing (section 11), rights in relation to automatic processing (section 12), rights to compensation in certain circumstances (section 13), rights for rectification, blocking and erasure (section 14) and the rights for an assessment (section 42). All these are explained in Chapter 4, The Scope of the Act, Chapter 6, Access to Personal Data and Chapter 13, Compliance.

It is worth noting here, however, that the principles and rights under this section are not mutually exclusive and each has to be read in conjunction with the others. It is quite possible that more than one will apply in a particular instance.

5.2.7   Principle 7 – Measures taken to keep information secure

Very simply, this principle means that the information must be kept secure. But what is secure? Consider the data and ask how sensitive it is. If it consists of just a name and address, then a locked building or room may do, but for financial data or health data a locked cabinet or encryption is essential.

Remember also that this is not just about storage. Leaving papers on the desk is a problem even if the office only has one occupant. What about people who visit the office when the occupant is not there and who could easily spot something highly confidential? Another problem is allowing computer screens to be seen through a window or reception desk. This is something that solicitors have to be aware of, using laptops on trains, allowing people around to see details of a couple's difficult divorce settlement is an easy mistake to make. In fact, this applies to anyone using laptops on public transport. The NHS has had many problems in the past with this principle, not only in the doctor's surgery where the illness of a patient can easily be disclosed to the whole waiting room, but also well-meaning actions, such as in the story below, which is an actual case.

A major hospital had a good idea to help patients at a special clinic for sexually transmitted diseases. They had an illuminated sign showing who was the next patient to be seen by the doctor. Unfortunately it was near the main hospital reception and could be seen by anyone entering the hospital.

Remember as well that keeping data secure can also refer to office gossip, such as: 'Did you hear that George in Accounts is filing for a divorce?' The story below gives an example of how even the most helpful of comments can lead to problems.

A member of staff was off sick with a stress-related illness and had only told the immediate members of his family as the situation was very sensitive. An aunt called the office to speak to the officer and was told by a colleague that he was off with stress. This caused a great deal of embarrassment in the family and added to the stress of the officer concerned.

This is the principle which can cause the most unintentional distress to a data subject, so it is important to be aware of the dangers and impress on others the need to only release as much information as is necessary.

5.2.8 Principle 8 – Not transferred outside the European Economic Area

This is the longest description of the principles and probably the one that most people think has little impact on them. However, this may not be the case.

The European Economic Area (EEA) includes the European Union and other countries, such as Switzerland and Norway. Data can be sent to

Europe, but what about elsewhere? Australia, Canada and New Zealand have strong laws, as has the Isle of Man, which was always the exception until recently. What about the United States of America? Here is a different story. Because of internal difficulty with industry America does not have strong data protection laws, although its freedom of information laws came in well before the United Kingdom's. It does, however, have safe harbor agreements with some organizations so that sharing can take place with them but not with the country as a whole. Sharing with the USA for immigration purposes is also permitted. India is trying to rush through similar laws because of the increasing use of Asian sites for call centres.

Data protection law is similar across Europe and the following story gives an example of how seriously the courts take this type of disclosure.

Remembering that data protection is European law, a major computer software company from the United States transferred its customer database from Barcelona to its headquarters in America without consent. The Spanish government fined it around £50,000 for having done so.

But information is not transferred outside Europe without consent – or is it? Just remember that many e-mail hosts are based in California. Never send anything relating to personal data on a postcard, and never send anything in an e-mail that you would not put on a postcard.

There are, however, nine examples of where sharing or transferring data abroad may apply lawfully and these are given at Schedule 4 of the Act.

> The subject has given his consent. (DPA 1998, Sch. 4(1))

As in other parts of the Act, consent has to be freely obtained.

> For the conclusion of a contract which is in the interests of the data subject or is at the request of the data subject. (DPA 1998, Sch. 4(2))

A clear example here would be a holiday arrangement in, say, Florida where it is necessary to share personal data in order that the accommodation can be booked.

3 The transfer is necessary:

(a) for the conclusion of a contract between the data controller and a person other than the data subject which –

(i) is entered into at the request of the data subject, or (ii) is in the interests of the data subject, or

(b) for the performance of such a contract.

(DPA 1998, Sch. 3)

Necessary in the substantial public interest.   (DPA 1998, Sch. 4(4))

This would be following a directive from the Secretary of State and has recently been applied in handing over the details of travellers to the United States to the US government as an anti-terrorism measure.

The usual exemption relating to

legal proceedings, legal advice and defending legal rights   (DPA 1998, Sch. 4(5))

can also be found. It has the same meaning here as has been examined earlier in this chapter. It also relates to paragraph 6, which refers to

vital interest.

Paragraph 7 is unusual as it is not specifically mentioned elsewhere in the principles.

Part of a public register subject to the register being open to inspection by the data subject.   (DPA 1998, Sch. 4(7))

This means that covert lists are not possible, but it would be argued that a public register is already available and published and so is in the public domain.

Paragraphs 8 and 9 require the Commissioner's approval and relate to the human rights of a subject,

are of a kind approved by the commission ensuring the safeguards for the rights
and freedoms of data subjects   (DPA 1998, Sch. 4(8))

and

the transfer has been approved by the commissioner in such a manner as to
ensure safeguards for the rights and freedoms of the data subject.

(DPA 1998, Sch. 4(9))

In these cases it is not necessary for the Commissioner to approve each case; he only needs to make the initial approval. Currently the European Union recognizes the following countries, outside the EEA, as having the adequacy of protection: Switzerland, Argentina, Guernsey, Isle of Man, USA (where a company has signed up to the safe harbor agreement), USA (transfer of passenger information) and Canada.

5.3   Summary

The eight principles are well listed at Schedule 1 of the Act and at Appendix 1 of this book, and form the backbone of all the data protection ideals. They are essential guidelines on how personal data should be handled, and on each occasion that personal data is processed some if not all of the exemptions must be considered.

It should be remembered that exemptions are not mutually exclusive and more than one may apply. The essential theme underlying these principles is the protection of the data subject, their statutory and implied rights of privacy and the right to ensure that data about them is processed lawfully.

When looking at data sharing all the principles must be considered as well as the other schedules of the Act, which explain the principles in more detail. As a basic rule of thumb, if all that is remembered about the Data Protection Act are the principles, then it is probable that most of the actions of the data controller will be compliant.

Having now established the principles to which you must work, the next major area of concern is that of access to data.

6

Access to personal data

6.1 Introduction

The rights of the individual to access personal data held about them are probably the most important element of the Data Protection Act. Access to third party data, while covered in this chapter, is also dealt with in Chapter 7 on data sharing. In this chapter we will be examining requests for data on a one-off basis, while in Chapter 7 we will look at sharing data on a regular basis.

It is important when considering access to establish under which legislation access is requested. To do this it is necessary to refer to the definitions of what is and what is not personal data explained in Chapter 3.

The first question to be asked is: 'Does the data requested relate to the individual who is requesting it or does it relate to someone else?' If the former, then it is relatively straightforward, as we shall see shortly; if the latter, many more safeguards and checks have to be observed.

6.2 Access to the data subject's personal data

6.2.1 Subject access request

Section 7 of the Act gives the data subject, the person whose data it is, the right of access to all data held by the data controller about that person (Section 7.1):

7 (1) Subject to the following provisions of this section and to sections 8 and 9 an individual is entitled –

(a) to be informed by any data controller whether personal data of which that individual is the data subject are being processed by or on behalf of that data controller,

(b) if that is the case, to be given by the data controller a description of –

(i)   the personal data of which that individual is the data subject,

(ii) the purposes for which they are being or are to be processed and

(iii) the recipients or classes of recipients to whom they are or may be disclosed.

(DPA 1998, s. 7(1))

These will be recognized as the requirements of the fair processing statement under the first data protection principle (see Chapter 5).

6.2.2   Scope of data to be released

Section 7 goes on to describe what information an individual must be supplied with when a request is made

(c) To have communicated to him in an intelligible form –

(i)   the information constituting any personal data of which that person is the data subject and

(ii) any information available to the data controller as to the source of that data.

(DPA 1998, s. 7(1))

According to these subsections, all the data held about an individual must be released to them, subject to the exemptions in the subsections that follow.

6.2.3   Intelligible format and automatic processed data

The information has to be provided in an intelligible form. This raises a number of interesting questions as to the definition of intelligible. If the person writes in English, then it is reasonable to assume that the answer can be given in English. If the request is to a Welsh authority, the requester may expect to receive the answer in Welsh. What about minority languages? It all depends on how the data is recorded and whether there is a requirement to keep it in a minority language; if so, there could then be an expectation to receive the information in that language. If not, it is possible that a translation of the data will not be expected, although this does not preclude an authority from providing one.

The matter of intelligible format applies also to information processed by automatic methods:

> (d) where the processing by automatic means of personal data of which that individual is the data subject for the purpose of evaluating matters relating to him such as, for example, his performance at work, his creditworthiness, his reliability or his conduct, has constituted or is likely to constitute the sole basis for any decision significantly affecting him, to be informed by the data controller of the logic involved in that decision-taking.
>
> (DPA 1998, s. 7(1))

This means that if data has been processed automatically, then the data subject must be told of the formula that was used and have this explained to him in a way that he can understand. It is insufficient to give a formula which is very complex and cannot be understood. This applies also to any abbreviations used, which must be explained. The following story shows how internal abbreviations must not be used, as it may be necessary to explain their meaning.

A housing authority used to have regular complainants and to warn staff of a frequent complainant it used the initials 'MOB' on the records. There was great embarrassment when a lady asked what this meant, following her request for data, and the manager had to state they stood for 'Moaning Old Biddy'.

6.2.4   Method of application

To obtain their data an individual must put in writing a request, pay the appropriate fee and also give some indication where the data is kept:

(2) A data controller is not obliged to supply any information under subsection (1) unless he has received –

   (a) a request in writing and

   (b) except in prescribed cases, such fee (not exceeding the prescribed maximum) as he may require.

(3) A data controller is not obliged to comply with a request under this section unless he is supplied with such information as he may reasonably require in order to satisfy himself as to the identity of the person making the request and to locate the information that person seeks.

(DPA 1998, s. 7(2))

The request must be in writing. E-mail is not sufficient because it is necessary to ensure that the subject is who he claims to be, and a signature and a return address that can be checked must be provided. The data controller cannot insist that the request is made on a pre-printed form, although to offer one is useful, provided that it enables the requester to be satisfactorily identified.

A data controller does not have to comply with a request if he is not satisfied as to the identity of the individual (section 7.3) or the location of the data. There is no requirement to ask for further proof of identity than a signature and return address. In fact this is frowned upon by the Information Commissioner. These will normally be sufficient proof but if there is any genuine doubt, then further proof, such as a driver's licence or passport, can be requested.

Of course not every one can make a request themselves: they may be too young, not speak English or simply want someone else to represent them. They should be asked to provide a form of authority (it could even be a letter from a solicitor) which gives consent for 'X' to represent them. If they cannot write, then a mark witnessed by an independent professional person will probably suffice. In the case of a minor it is necessary to know their age and their understanding of what they are asking for. This is known as Gillick Competencies, based on the decision in *Gillick* v. *West Norfolk and Wisbech Area Health Authority* [1985]. This case established that it is necessary to test the understanding of the child to make sure they know what they are authorising. England and Wales does not have a statutory age for giving authority. In Scotland it is 12 years, and this example can be followed, so individuals aged 12 years and over can make their own requests with help from a responsible adult. With under–12s it is necessary to make sure the child's representative has parental responsibility and is actually acting in their best interest. There is no requirement to release to a third party, so a request can be refused if the data controller is not satisfied as to the representation. A request made by a third party on behalf of the subject is as though the subject themself has made the request and this is how the remainder of the process must be handled.

The fee is covered below in section 6.2.5. As regards the location of the data, it is not a requirement that the subject knows the exact location of their data, but to request all of the information an organization holds about them is also not enough. All that is needed is for the requester to give some indication as to the location of the data. Comments such as 'all my housing records' or 'my personnel and supervisory files' will usually suffice. If the subject is requesting e-mails, then it is reasonable to ask for the mailbox name and the time period to be stated. 'All e-mails about me received or sent by Joe Smith over the past six months' would probably be sufficient.

6.2.5   Fees

Section 7.2 also indicates that a fee may be payable. The amount of the fees is laid down in the fee regulations SI 2000/191. To charge a fee is not compulsory, and in fact a number of public authorities do not charge because the cost of raising an invoice is more than the prescribed fee. At least one authority requires the requester to send in a cheque with the request and returns the cheque with the papers that have been found on the individual. This is done to prevent frivolous requests. At current (2007) levels the standard maximum fee for records kept in a recognized filing system is £10; because it is a statutory charge VAT does not apply. Access to school records is free unless the requester wants a copy, for which the fee is £1 per 10 pages up to 100 pages and then £5 per 50 pages up to a maximum charge of £50 (SI 2000/191). School records are as defined under the Education Acts and are those kept by the school. The same scales of fees apply to medical records. For records kept by credit reference agencies the fee is £2.50. These charges are to cover all expenses, and extra charges cannot be made for copying except in the cases of school and medical records. At the time of writing, the government has no intention to amend these fees. The statutory time (not exceeding 40 days) within which the data must be delivered to the requester does not start to run until the data controller has received the fees. In practice, this means that the time starts when the fee has been cleared through the bank.

These fees do not apply to unstructured data (data not held in a relevant filing system as defined in section 1(1) of the Data Protection Act) held by a public authority. Such records are accessible but section 9A of the Act (amended by the Freedom of Information Act 2000 section 69) states that files held in an unstructured manner do not have to be supplied if the costs of doing so would exceed the appropriate limit of the fees:

> (3) Even if the data are described by the data subject in his request, a public authority is not obliged to comply with subsection (1) of section 7 in relation to unstructured personal data if the authority estimates that the cost of complying with the request so far as relating to those data would exceed the appropriate limit.   (DPA 1998, s. 9A(3))

This amendment brings unstructured data into line with the freedom of information rules and if it will cost more than £600 for a request to central government or £450 for any other authority, the request need not be complied with. This figure is calculated at a rate of £25 an hour, which works out at roughly 2½ days of work for non central government authorities. Under this there will not be a fee applicable although if it costs more than the appropriate limit (£600, or £450 at £25 per hour) to find the data, then the whole time can be taken into account.

6.3   Access to third party data

The rest of section 7 refers to access to data about another person, known as third party data. A third party can be anyone other than the requester, e.g. child, parent, sibling, solicitor or friend.

If it is found that the data requested contains references to another person, the easiest thing to do is to remove from the data everything about the third party (known as redaction). However, there are a number of considerations to be taken into account. Does the requester know about the third party and about the facts that are being reported? If the subject was at a meeting where items relating to another person were discussed, then it can safely be assumed that the requester knows about the details relating to that person. It would be unnecessary to remove the information and to do so could lead to the subject claiming that data was being withheld.

With other information about a third party there are still some questions to be asked. Is the information generally well known or already published (for example in a newspaper report), or can the person be readily contacted to find out if they consent to its release? Another consideration with regard to the latter point is that by contacting the third party to ask for release they are being told that someone has requested the data and this could cause them considerable damage or distress. The Act goes on to explain the four points that should be considered when identifying third party data:

(6) (a) any duty of confidentiality owed to the other individual,

(b) any steps taken by the data controller with a view to seeking the consent of the other individual,

(c) whether the other individual is capable of giving consent, and

(d) any express refusal of consent by the other individual.

(DPA 1998, s. 7(6))

From this it can be seen that the third party's rights must also be protected and this section does place an obligation on the data controller to attempt to contact the individual unless there are reasons for not doing so. It may not be possible to contact the individual; also it may not be possible for them to give consent freely. All these factors must be taken into account. If the individual refuses consent it must be considered whether this consent was unreasonably withheld. If this is the case it may constitute good grounds for releasing the data.

Access to birth parent details and to other information contained in adoption matters is covered by the Children and Adoption Act 2002 and does not come under the Data Protection Act so the above rules do not apply.

It is interesting to note that the Act states that third party consent must be obtained promptly and definitely within the 40 days. As a rough guide in dealing with third party data, the principle of 'If in doubt, take it out' is usually adopted. At least that way no one will be hurt by the unwanted release of information.

The names of professional persons carrying out their duties should be left in (i.e. not redacted) unless to do so would cause them damage or distress. This is covered by Schedule 12 and by Statutory Instruments 2000/413, 414 and 415, which relate to health, education and social service records.

Schedule 12 allows housing and social work records, even if they are unstructured, to come under the main provisions of the Act, so section 9A relating to unstructured data (see above, 6.2.5) does not apply to this data. They are described as 'accessible records'.

6.4   Exemptions to section 7 requests

There are always exceptions to the rule. Section 8 lists some circumstances in which a request need not be complied with.

Section 8(2) states that data must be released in a permanent form and in a way in which the requester can understand it, unless:

2(a)   the supply of such a copy is not possible or would involve disproportionate effort or

(b)   the data subject agrees otherwise.

And where any of the information referred to in section 7(1)(c)(i) is expressed in terms which are not intelligible without explanation the copy must be accompanied by an explanation of those terms.   (DPA 1998, s. 8(2))

Section 7(1)(c)(i) is a normal subject access request.

6.4.1   Disproportionate effort

If it will take too long and cost too much to photocopy the data, then it is possible to claim this exemption. However, it may be considered that an individual who wants to see his very extensive social work file has a genuine need, in which case this exemption may be waived. Subsection 2(a) covers again the point made above (see paragraph 6.3) that the redaction must be explained to the requester.

6.4.2   Same or similar requests

Has the requester made the same or similar request recently? If so, section 8(3) states that the data controller does not have to search again:

> Where a data controller has previously complied with a request made under section 7 by an individual, the data controller is not obliged to comply with a subsequent identical or similar request by that individual unless a reasonable interval has elapsed between compliance with the previous request and the making of the current request.   (DPA 1998, s. 8(3))

The data controller should consider the frequency of change of the data and if it has not changed should use this exemption, although he must also consider the reasons why the data was collected. If it has changed, he only needs to release the new material.

6.4.3   Trade secrets

If the information gives away a trade secret, the data does not need to be released. This is covered by section 8(5) which says the section of the Act (7(1)(d)) that permits access to data

> is not to be regarded as requiring the provision as to the logic involved in the decision taking if, and to the extent that, the information constitutes a trade secret.   (DPA 1998, s. 8(5))

This means that any information that could be classed as commercially confidential and could have a detrimental effect on the commercial operation of an organization or another need not be released. Care must be taken in applying this exemption, as it must be proved that actual damage would occur if the data were released.

6.4.4 Information prepared after a request

Any information which has been created after the receipt of a request does not have to be released (section 8(6)). The requested information is supplied as at the date of receipt (this provision applies under all three of the information Acts). Obviously, this does not preclude the release of data prepared after the date of the request but it can be useful, in the case of ongoing work, that comments about the request do not have to be released until a further request for information is made. Remember that if additional information has been generated, this does not come under the heading of a repeated request.

6.4.5 Credit reference agencies

Section 9 of the Act assumes that if a subject requests data from a credit reference agency they only want data relevant to their financial standing, unless they state otherwise.

Release of information under section 7 of the Act (access to data) is also controlled, in the case of credit reference agencies, by section 159 of the Consumer Credit Act 1974, and information must be supplied in accordance with that legislation.

6.4.6 Confidential references

Confidential references can be exempt, although most companies and authorities do release them and tell referees that this is their policy. If an organization does decide to release references, then this decision must apply to all requests and a reference cannot be withheld just because the requester is not liked. Schedule 7 adds some further exemptions:

Schedule 7

1 Personal data are exempt from section 7 if they consist of a reference given or
   to be given in confidence by the data controller for the purposes of

   (a) the education, training or employment, or prospective education, training
       or employment, of the data subject,

   (b) the appointment, or prospective appointment, of the data subject to any
       office, or

   (c)   the provision, or prospective provision, by the data subject of any service.

                                                                    (DPA 1998, Sch. 7)

6.4.7   Armed forces, judicial appointments and honours

Where release of information would prejudice the effectiveness of the
armed forces it is exempt from disclosure, as is information on judicial
appointments and honours. This includes judicial office or appointments
to Queen's Counsel (QC).

   [Schedule 7, paragraphs 2, 3 and 4.]

6.4.8   Management forecasts

Management forecasting and planning are exempt, but only to the extent
that they would prejudice the conduct of a business. This would have to
be a provable prejudice, as in the case of appointments or potential
dismissal, not merely something that would be inconvenient to the
company. While the forecast or plans are being made it may be possible to
argue that the information should be withheld, but once the decision has
been made then it would be difficult to rely on this exemption.

   Schedule 7 adds some further exemptions:

5 Personal data processed for the purposes of management forecasting or
management planning to assist the data controller in the conduct of any business
or other activity are exempt from the subject information provisions in any case
to the extent to which the application of those provisions would be likely to
prejudice the conduct of that business or other activity.

                                                                    (DPA 1998, Sch. 7)

6.4.9   Corporate finance

Schedule 7 contains quite a long exemption but the following attempts to reduce it somewhat so that it can be more easily understood. Personal data processed by a corporate finance service need not be disclosed if:

(a) (i) the application of those provisions to the data controller could affect the price of any instrument which is already in existence or is to be or may be created, or

(ii) the data controller reasonably believes that the application of those provisions to the data could affect the price of such an instrument, and

(b) to the extent that the data are not exempt from the subject information provisions by virtue of paragraph (a), they are exempt from those provisions if the exemption is required for the purpose of safeguarding an important economic or financial interest of the United Kingdom.

(DPA 1998, Sch. 7(6))

Thus for the first part to apply the financial interests of the UK must be safeguarded by withholding information where pricing may be affected. The Secretary of State can issue an order to give guidance on what can or cannot be taken into account.

6.4.10 Negotiations

Ongoing negotiations constitute an exemption if the release of information would prejudice the outcome. However, the information may not be exempt after the negotiations have been completed. This exemption could apply to any sort of negotiations, even relating to disciplinary action if the release of data would prejudice an investigation. As soon as the release of information ceases to be a threat, however, the information can be released.

6.4.11 Examination marks

Examination marks are exempt from release for five months from the date of the request for information if that is made before the publication date or within 40 days of the results being published, whichever is the earlier. Examination scripts are also exempt if they contain personal data; remember, however, that the information has to be personal and about a living individual. This could include data written by an examiner which reveals information or an opinion about the candidate. In at least one university it is known that examiners have to write on separate sheets so their comments can be released.

Examinations are defined as

> any process for determining the knowledge, intelligence, skill or ability of a candidate by reference to his performance in any test, work or other activity.
>
> (DPA 1998, Sch. 7(8))

The exemption therefore covers tests for appraisals and interviews as well as educational examinations.

6.4.12 Legal privilege

Legal professional privilege is exempt. Remember we are still talking of personal data, for under freedom of information these comments are subject to a public interest test. For information to be covered by legal privilege it has to be relating to opinion or advice in litigation and not just a request for a meeting unless that would give away any legal opinion. This section is to protect the confidentiality between the lawyer and the client:

> 10 Personal data are exempt from the subject information provisions if the data consist of information in respect of which a claim to legal professional privilege or, in Scotland, to confidentiality between client and professional legal adviser, could be maintained in legal proceedings.   (DPA 1998, Sch. 7(10))

6.4.13 Self incrimination

This exemption can be applied if the information released under a section 7 request could be used against the data controller in a criminal court. Similarly if data reveals that an offence has been committed under the

Data Protection Act, this cannot be used in evidence if it was obtained under a section 7 request. Of course, if such data were released under a section 7 request there would be nothing to prevent a similar request being made for the same data under other legislation, which could then be used in court.

6.5   Access for crime prevention, detection and taxation

A well-used (although not always correctly) section of the Act, section 29, allows exemption from the non disclosure provisions for the purposes of detection, prevention of crime, apprehension, prosecution of offenders and assessment or collection of tax, duty or similar imposition. In such cases the data controller has to be satisfied that the requesting officer has the power to make such a request. What is the crime; is the request directed at a specific individual or group of individuals and not just a general investigation, are other questions that need to be addressed.

For police requests, the requesting officer should apply on a specific form which has been approved by Association of Chief Police Officers (ACPO). The form should be signed by the requesting officer and will provide answers to both the above questions. The form should be countersigned by an officer of the rank of inspector or above.

Requests for information under section 29 are not restricted to the police; other regular requesters are immigration officials and the Child Support Agency (CSA), in fact any organization which has the authority to investigate a crime. If an organization wishes to use section 29 to obtain information for its own investigations it should devise a simple form which should state that it requires information under section 29(3) of the Data Protection Act, the crime being investigated and who is being investigated. In the case of organizations other than the police the form should also state the legislation that relates to the crime.

There are two things to remember. The Data Protection Act does not give consent to sharing, it is other relevant legislation which gives this so, 'I want to share under the Data Protection Act' is simply not valid. And the Act does not create a compulsion to share, only permission. The data controller still has to comply with the conditions laid down in Schedule 2, and ask 'is it lawful'? If in any doubt, do not share. It is worth bearing in mind that data incorrectly obtained may be thrown out of court as unlawful, so it is in everyone's interest that the forms are correct.

In a case of child abuse information was obtained by the police without the necessary paperwork and the judge deemed it inadmissible in court. The prosecution was relying on this paperwork as primary evidence, and so the case was lost.

Under the tax provisions trawling is permitted, although again a signed document should be retained to show that access was lawfully given. The forms issued by HM Revenue and Customs are a good example of how a tax request should be made, as they explain the requirements and the law.

Finally remember the investigation has to be into a criminal offence or for tax purposes and cannot include council tax data that contains a name because to share this is unlawful under the Local Government Finance Act 1992 Sch. 2(17) and (18). Even the Information Commissioner in his guidelines states that council tax data cannot be used if other legislation prohibits its being shared.

6.6 Access by health, education and social work professionals

Occasionally it is necessary for those working in health, education and social work to access files about individuals held by other authorities without obtaining the consent of the subject. In order to assess whether a child can stay with a parent it may be necessary to look at the social care file of a new partner, to judge whether the child will be safe there.

This is covered in the Data Protection Act at section 30, which allows the Secretary of State to raise an order allowing this to happen. These orders were raised in 2000, through Statutory Instruments 2000/413, 2000/414 and 2000/415. These allow sharing of information without consent if it is for the benefit of the data subject or others. The request must come from a professional working in the specific area, say social work, and be, in this case, for the social well-being and care of the data subject or others. The request must be in writing and the data controller should always make sure that it is from a relevant professional and that it is for the benefit of the subject or others.

Health professionals are defined under section 69 as being

(a) a registered medical practitioner

(b) a registered dentist

(c) a registered optician

(d) a registered pharmaceutical chemist

(e) a registered nurse, midwife or health visitor

(f) a registered osteopath

(g) a registered chiropractor

(h) any person who is registered as a member of a profession to which the Professions Supplementary to Medical Act 1960 for the time being exists

(i) a clinical psychologist, child psychotherapist or speech therapist

(j) a music therapist employed by a health service body and

(k) a scientist employed by such a body as head of department.

(DPA 1998, s. 69)

6.7   Regulatory exemptions

Section 31 is an interesting catchall for those areas that do not come within section 29, which covers criminal matters; sections 31 and 35 cover civil matters. Section 31 states that data can be exempt from the non disclosure provisions if it would be likely to prejudice the discharge of the following functions were the data not released:

2(a) for protecting members of the public against

(i) financial loss due to dishonesty, malpractice or other serious improper conduct by, or the unfitness or incompetence of, persons concerned in the provision of banking, insurance, investment or other financial services or in the management of bodies corporate

(ii) financial loss due to the conduct of discharge or undischarge of bankrupts or

(lii) dishonesty, malpractice or other serious improper conduct by, or the
unfitness or incompetence of persons authorised to carry on any
profession or activity.

(DPA 1998, s. 31)

The remainder of section 31 applies to protecting charities and securing
the health, safety and welfare of people at work. To request access under
section 31 the requester would need to convince the data controller that
these conditions did apply. Again, if there is any doubt, the advice would
be not to release the data.

These provisions apply to any work that is carried out that

is of a public nature and in the exercise of the public interest.   (DPA 1998, s. 31)

It is interesting to note the general absence of public interest references in
this Act, as opposed to the other two enactments in the information rights
trilogy, which will be examined in later chapters.

Trading standards functions also come under section 31(5) making
them exempt from the non disclosure provisions where non disclosure of
data would prejudice any investigations being carried out. Again, requests
for access should be in writing, making sure the relevant legislation is well
specified.

6.8   Journalism, literature and art

The second of the Act's rare references to public interest occurs in section
32. Personal data requested for journalism, literature and art can be
released under section 32, but only if

the data controller reasonably believes that, having regard in particular to the
special importance of the public interest in the freedom of expression, publication
would be in the public interest, and c) the data controller reasonably believes that
in all the circumstances, compliance with that provision is incompatible with the
special purpose.

(DPA 1998, s. 32)

The subject of public interest will be looked at later in Chapter 11, but remember that what is of interest to the public is not necessarily in the public interest. An example of data released in the public interest would be information about expenses claimed by an elected person, indicating how public funds are spent. This is a very imprecise section using words such as 'reasonably' and 'in all circumstances', but it simply means that the application of the public interest test needs to be justified and if it can be applied it will probably be in compliance.

The exemption applies to all the principles except principle 7, which means that the data still has to be kept secure.

6.9   Research, history and statistics

Section 33, headed 'Research, History and Statistics', states that research includes that done for statistical and historical purposes. The best approach would be to depersonalize the information. Indeed, when the results of any research are published they must be depersonalized. Information can be collected for research purposes without consent if the results do not identify any individual. This is easy when large numbers are involved but not so straightforward in the case of small numbers, as can be seen in the following example.

Lowmoor Road has a great many houses and 20% of the occupants are Greek. As there are a few hundred residents in the road this information does not identify anyone. However, for an office of 50 people, to specify that 2% of staff have an illness could identify an individual, because 2% of 50 is 1.

It is suggested that in statistical research involving small numbers, if the result is less than 10%, then say 'less than 10%' rather than giving an exact figure, to protect the identity of individuals.

6.10   Already available to the public or by enactment

Section 34 states the obvious: if data is already in the public domain it can be released. This is often the defence in cases involving celebrities, as it is claimed that their information is already available, and was the argument in the case of *Douglas and others* v. *Hello! Ltd* [2001] (see Chapter 2.1). If another Act makes the information public, this also constitutes being in the public domain. This is an interesting argument when discussing names and dates of birth, because the birth registers are a public record under the Births and Deaths Registration Act 1953. However, this depends on ease of access to the records. It is clear that the requester has to be able to access them easily. If not, for example if they live abroad, it may be advisable to send a copy to them.

6.11 Disclosures required by law and the courts

Section 35 states that personal data is exempt from the non disclosure provisions if

1) . . . the disclosure is required by or under any enactment, by any rule of law or by the order of a court.
2) . . . a) for the purposes of, or in connection with, any legal proceedings (including prospective legal proceedings), or

   b) for the purpose of obtaining legal advice, or is otherwise necessary for the purposes of establishing, exercising or defending legal rights.

(DPA 1998, s. 35)

This does not, however, mean that all the available data has to be released. Even with a court order only information that is relevant to the matter at hand should be released. Most large authorities have specialist disclosure officers to handle such requests or send the papers to barristers to establish what is relevant. Family and civil courts can get very upset if papers prepared for them are released to the Crown Court. However, there is a directive from the Lord Chancellor in 2006 which allows family matters to be given to child care professionals, and this includes the child abuse and paedophiliac teams of the local police, without reference to the Court. Otherwise the court must always be asked for consent first, although it is not always given, at least not in its entirety. This can be overcome with prearranged protocols, such as in the following example.

It is interesting that experiments are being carried out in some places with a more direct method, known in some places as Annex B, for release of third party information without consent in child abuse cases. This experiment involves a protocol between the local authorities, the police and the Crown Prosecution Service (CPS) that a special form will be issued by the police to the local authority at the point of arrest. The prosecution case and, when available, the defence case are given to the authority to assist with the purpose of disclosure, and the police, the authority or counsel will look for disclosure issues in the papers before the case progresses. This way the local authority can assess whether the public interest immunities test needs to be carried out at an early stage and this can be done with the cooperation of all the parties.

There is also pressure to apply this type of protocol to matters such as murder, rape and serious assault and to extend this trial around the country. The Children Act 2004 and the Education Act 2002 can help to allow this sort of exchange if applied carefully.

If there is no such agreement or there are other issues it is advisable that a court order or witness order is obtained before release and remembering that, without one, there is no obligation to release and even then only the information which can be used in evidence and is relevant to the case should be given. If there is any dispute the court, through the judge, will ask to see all the papers and agree with the public authority what can be disclosed.

6.12   Domestic and recreational purposes

Personal data for purely private uses, such as card lists for birthdays and festivals are all exempt, even from the data protection principles. Section 36 states:

> Personal data processed by an individual only for purposes of that individual's personal, family or household affairs (including recreational purposes) are exempt from the data protection principles and the provisions of Parts II and III.
>
> (DPA 1998, s. 36)

All data processing that is done purely for domestic use falls outside the Act and is not of any concern.

6.13   Summary

The most important parts of the Data Protection Act, after establishing what is personal data, are those relating to access.

Access to personal data is a somewhat complex area. There are many elements that must be taken into account in order for a data subject to be given access to data; there is often a misunderstanding of what can be released and what cannot. It is important that the definition of personal data is understood, especially if the data contains information about another person.

A data subject can be given almost all information owned by an organization that relates to the subject, including opinions. In fact, as has been seen in this chapter, it is mainly information about the subject that might affect other processes, or forms part of legal opinion, which can be withheld.

Access by third parties on a one-off basis is also carefully controlled, and care must be taken before information is released that it does not contain information about other people unless permitted.

Access can be obtained to third party data in certain circumstances, but again there has to be a specific reference to this type of access in the Data Protection Act to allow this type of information to be given. While the Act does not give specific authority to release such information, it does give exemptions to the non disclosure provisions.

There are, however, other times when access to data is needed other than on a one-off basis. If it is required on a regular basis, then this is covered by data sharing, which forms the basis of the next chapter.

7

Data sharing

7.1   Introduction

When the Data Protection Act first came out it was seen by many as a barrier to data sharing. In fact even now there are many cases when we hear 'We can't tell you that because of data protection'. The non disclosure provisions of the Act were seen as restricting access and no account was taken of the many exemptions to these provisions, some of which were considered earlier in Chapter 6.

This chapter will examine how the Act protects personal data but does, in almost every case, allow sharing of data with third parties for legitimate purposes.

7.2   The guidelines

A few specific questions should be asked before sharing can take place. Provided that the answers are affirmative, then sharing is no problem.

The first question is: 'Has the data subject given consent?' This is particularly important if the data is sensitive and falls under a Schedule 3 condition (see Chapter 3.7). As was mentioned earlier, it is essential that specific consent is given by the data subject, stating that the subject agrees to the data being shared with a third party for another purpose.

If the data does not come under Schedule 3, i.e. it is non sensitive personal data, then consent is desirable but not essential, although it is important to inform the subject about the sharing. There is a requirement to issue a fair processing statement telling the subject how the data will be used and with whom it will be shared. This does not have to be too specific:

'Your information will be shared with other areas of this authority for the purpose of providing other services to which you have already agreed and as required by law.'

This statement should also be included in the notification to the Information Commissioner that personal data is being processed (see Chapter 4.8). The individual has to be made aware of the purpose of the data sharing and with whom the data is being shared, although again a general approach is acceptable, such as 'shared with voluntary sector' rather than 'XYZ Charity', which is very specific. Remember that in most cases an individual can withdraw consent to data sharing, so systems must be in place to ensure that this can be handled promptly. Finally, note that an individual cannot give consent to an unlawful act, so if there is any legislation that prohibits data sharing, consent does not provide a way around this. For regulation 5 of the Environmental Information Regulations, which overrides any other legislation prohibiting sharing, see paragraph 10.2.24, Chapter 10.

The next question is: 'What is the law that permits the data to be shared?' Everything that public sector authorities do is controlled by one law or another, so there should be a law that permits sharing. It could be the Crime and Disorder Act 1998, for the detection or prevention of crime. For Local Authorities the Local Government Act 2000 section 2 is useful as it allows councils to do things for the benefit of the community. Among the various children's acts the Children and Adoption Act 2002 in particular concerns sharing for the benefit of a child. Each area of the public sector has its own Acts and the staff working in the specialist areas should know the legislation that is applicable. Anyone who is asked to share data should always check under what legislation the other party is operating.

Remember that there may be legislation that prohibits data sharing. As stated in paragraph 5.2.1, Chapter 5, the Local Government Finance Act 1992 restricts the use of council tax data, where even the consent of the data subject is insufficient. Other legislation that restricts sharing includes the Enterprise Act 2002, which relates in the main to investigations such as trading standards offices might carry out, and the Finance Act 1988, which relates to the use of income tax data. In these cases it can even be an imprisonable offence to share data. The Social Security Administration Act 1992 also requires consent for sharing of data relating to housing and council tax benefits, except in matters relating to the detection or prevention of crime and the apprehension or prosecution of offenders.

If data sharing is requested, it is advisable not to agree unless the other party can explain why the data is needed and specify the legislation that relates to the sharing. The Data Protection Act itself does not give consent to sharing data; all that this Act does is provide exemptions from the non disclosure provisions of the Act. There is still a requirement for the sharing to be lawful (principle 1 of the Act).

This leads on to the subject of protocols, and it should be asked whether there is a data sharing protocol in place and whether the sharing is in line with its requirements.

7.3   Protocols

There is no requirement in law to have a protocol. That does not mean there should not be one, or that they do not have their uses. If the sharing is one-off or very infrequent a protocol is not much use. However, if it is necessary to share on a regular basis, a protocol sets down the principles for sharing, who owns the data and why it is being shared, as well as other details. It enables everyone to know what they can and should be doing with the data.

Consider who is going to use the protocol. It needs to be a comprehensive but concise and plain English document that informs the staff who do the job what they should be doing. It is recommended to organize it into different levels of detail so that those doing the job can easily turn to the relevant sections. This model suggests a pyramid, with an overall agreement at the beginning and below that the actual details of sharing.

The top level is a statement of intent by the top management. It is always wise to get the chief executive, chief constable, vice chancellor etc. to sign this document, as it then commits the whole authority to the principles and gives them corporate backing. Local protocols are fine, but rather than the police making separate agreements, which probably say the same thing, with social services and with education, it is much better to have an overall policy signed by the head of paid service that covers the entire organization. Within this there should be a statement of intent that will show how each partner will work towards more effective data sharing and state the overall objectives of sharing. Below are suggested details to be included in the protocol.

The legal constraints to sharing

There are certain laws which may cover all of the sharing that is intended: Data Protection Act 1998, Crime and Disorder Act 1998, Local Government Act 2000, Children and Adoptions Act 2002 are just some that may be applicable. Consideration should also be given to legislation that prohibits sharing: Finance Act 1998, Local Government Finance Act 1992 and Enterprise Act 2000 for example.

Any general restrictions that may apply should also be listed. An example could be that e-mail attachments will only be sent to secure sites such as GSI (Government Secure Internet), police and other law enforcement sites, or only to .gov sites – each of these is within a closed network and as such is considerably safer than normal internet sites.

Systems in place if things go wrong

This section will include a complaints procedure and will also show who will investigate and what the penalties are if the agreements are breached. An example of a penalty would be that sharing with a particular partner would stop until security was improved.

Data ownership

When data is shared between organizations it usually remains in the ownership of the originator and this needs to be taken into account when requests are received for personal data under section 7 of the Data

Protection Act 1998 or under the Freedom of Information Act 2000 or Environmental Information Regulations 2004. When the request relates to information held by a public authority, not only that owned by the authority, the protocol should remind partners of the duty under section 16 of the Freedom of Information Act 2000 to consult the originator before the information is released.

Security of the data

This will vary depending on the individual levels of sensitivity of the data. For example, health data will have a much greater level of security than, say, a list of contacts with voluntary authorities. In fact some protocols direct that sharing will not take place unless certain measures are introduced by all partners to ensure adequate security. Do not forget the other essential data protection requirement, 'that data can only be used for the purpose(s) it was supplied'. It should be stated in the protocol that:

'Data shared will only be used for the purposes as described in the protocol and for no other purpose except as required by law or with the agreement of the originating partner.'

The primary partners

The primary partners may want to be listed at this stage, but it is sometimes preferable to refer to an attached schedule, which makes it easier to add new partners at a later stage. A simple statement such as the following may suffice.

'This agreement is between Umbridgeshire Police and the Umbridge City Council and any other partners as shown at Appendix One who shall be jointly agreed by the two primary partners.'

Some protocol templates are available, notably one suggested by the Ministry of Justice (www.justice.gov.uk/docs/data_sharing_legal_guidance. pdf); some are obtainable from professional associations such as

Association of Chief Police Officers (ACPO) or National Association for Information Management (NAIM).

This overarching protocol will, by necessity, be somewhat longer than the lower levels. However, the issues covered will not be repeated at the operational levels. Indeed, it is recommended that the general principles are only referenced at the second level, because the operational protocols have a different purpose.

The operational protocol

The purpose of the operational protocol is to inform those who actually do the sharing on a daily basis how it is to be done. It does not need to be signed off by the chief officer, but can be signed off at a lower level relating to a specific operation. The operational protocol could relate to data sharing for prevention of antisocial behaviour, partnerships for reduction in drugs use, or even the smooth preparation of information for court in specific cases such as child abuse issues.

The operational protocol will start with a statement of the objectives for information sharing. This need be no longer than one paragraph but should refer back to the overarching agreement. It could even be under the heading 'Objective':

'Objective – To share personal data about our respective service users/customers to ensure a greater continuation and improvement of service to them', or 'Objective – to reduce the amount of debt incurred by public authorities'.

The partners

The partners relevant at the operational level should be listed. Refer to the authority at its highest level so that the protocol encompasses everyone.

Rather than stating that the agreement is between, for example, ''C' Division of Umbridgeshire Police and the Education Department's Admissions team', use the much more straightforward and all-encompassing 'Umbridgeshire Police and the Umbridge City Council'.

The legal basis for sharing

The specific legislation that permits sharing in each area should be listed, but without going into too much detail. If someone needs to know the details they can look them up. Avoid referring to sections of Acts as this would restrict the application of the protocol. Remember, for example, that data sharing can occur under a number of different sections of an Act, as already seen in Data Protection Act sections 7, 8, 29, 30, 31 and 35, to list a few (see Chapter 6).

Updating and retention of data

Information will be continually changing and a system should be in place to ensure that all partners are informed when data changes. This will be different for each type of data and as it is an operational matter it should be mentioned at this level. It is also necessary to agree how long the data will be kept. A bland statement that it will be kept as long as necessary is not sufficient. A more detailed declaration is needed, with reference to individual partners' retention schedules (refer to Chapter 15 for explanation). There may also be further restrictions. For example, the partners may agree that when the purpose for which the data has been shared has been fulfilled the original data will be returned to the supplying partner and all other copies destroyed. The following statement could be useful:

'Shared data will be kept in accordance with the supplying partner's retention guidelines and will, in any event, not be kept for longer than is required for the purposes of the sharing partner, when it will be disposed of in a secure manner or returned to the supplying partner.'

The method of sharing

This section should describe the process of sharing. Is it necessary for a form to be filled in each time sharing is required? If yes, the form should be described and the means of authorization specified. A log should be kept to provide an audit trail of how the data is being shared.

The detailed sections of the protocol should be clear and easily understood by those who will be doing the sharing. It should therefore not be too legal in tone. While it should aim to cover most eventualities it should not be so long as to discourage reading. The document should be easily referenced so that it is not necessary to read the whole agreement just to find the bit that is needed.

7.4   Summary

The purpose of the Data Protection Act is not to prohibit sharing of data provided that it is done lawfully and with the security and rights of individuals taken into account. In fact if used properly the Act actually promotes data sharing and will enable data to be shared in such a way that it can be used in the courts, or to avoid any litigation for breach of privacy. The primary objective in data sharing must be the protection and the benefit of the data subject, so sharing cannot be done just because it seems to be a good idea. There must be legal grounds for sharing by an organization, and great care has to be taken if the sharing is for commercial benefit.

While there is no requirement to have a protocol it is certainly very useful as a guide for staff who need to share data. It can also be used as a reference if the purpose for sharing is challenged. A number of protocols are being drafted that are generally relevant across the country and it is always a good idea to do some research to find if there is already a similar document in existence. Standardized protocols, which may differ in content at the second stage because they relate to specific projects, are also very useful because they enable authorities that cover larger geographical areas to have similar agreements across their territory. As well as making exchange across large areas easier, the sharing also becomes less complex if staff, e.g. police officers, have to share with a number of smaller geographical areas, such as district councils.

In the chapters that follow the Data Protection Act is placed into the background and you will be introduced to the other two pieces of legislation that make up the information rights trilogy.

8

The Freedom of Information Act 2000 and Environmental Information Regulations 2004, SI 2004/3391

8.1 Introduction

So far we have looked at personal data and this still needs to be kept in mind while we examine the next two enactments. With these, however, the main objective is the release of information rather than the security and handling of the information. In later chapters we will also need to examine some of the additional elements such as records management, public registers and the way in which environmental data is stored.

Each of the three pieces of legislation is unique and at the same time shares many common features with the others. The Data Protection Act is unique in that it describes not just how data is accessed but also how data is collected, kept and used. This Act is the only one that relates to everyone, not just to the public sector.

The Freedom of Information Act 2000 is unique in that it is the only Act of the three not based directly on European law. There is also a separate Freedom of Information Act in Scotland (Freedom of Information (Scotland) Act 2002), which has the same basic provisions but in which the sections come in a different order. The references to sections in these chapters are to the England, Northern Ireland and Wales Act.

The Environmental Information Regulations 2004 are unique in that they are a statutory instrument and not a primary Act and the only one of the information rights trilogy that does not permit other legislation to take precedence. This will be explained in Chapters 9 and 10.

In this chapter it is intended to give a brief overview of the Freedom of Information Act 2000 and the Environmental Information Regulations 2004, with the detail being studied in more depth in the following chapters.

8.2   The Freedom of Information Act 2000

The Freedom of Information Act 2000 was enacted to allow access to public sector information. There is a presumption within the Act, therefore, that information will be released, although there are 26 instances when disclosure can be disallowed (these are explained in detail in Chapter 10).

Every single request for information that a public authority receives in writing is, in law, a Freedom of Information Act request. If the request relates to personal data, then the exemption at section 40 for personal data should apply and it should be handled under the Data Protection Act and if it is for information relating to the environment, then section 39 is involved, which states that it should be dealt with under Environmental Information Regulations. Obviously it is not practical to reject every request which comes under other legislation and then state that it will be handled under the separate enactment, but this does illustrate the catch-all provisions of the Act.

The Act, while unlike its sister legislation not based on European law, has been seen as a change in culture for the public sector. No longer can disclosure be left to the discretion of the public authority; there are strict guidelines as to how information should be released. However, it does enable public authorities to be more open and accountable and, if applied properly, should dispose of the perception of secrecy.

That having been said, it is accepted that there have been cases of abuse of the system and the government is continually seeking to make amendments to reduce any abuse. The main concern that was initially expressed related to commercial requests for information which certain companies then used for their own profit. It is worth remembering the Re-use of Public Sector Information Regulations 2005 and even copyright law when handling some of these requests. These regulations will be explained more fully in Chapter 17.5.

The time limits for fulfilling Freedom of Information requests are similar to those of the Environmental Information Regulations but are completely different from those of the Data Protection Act; these will be explained in Chapter 9.

8.3   The Environmental Information Regulations 2004, SI 2004/3391

These are described by some as the Cinderella of information rights legislation, as they seem to sit in the shadow of freedom of information, while having more power than the Freedom of Information Act and being based on European law (Directive (EC) 2003/4(d)). There have been environmental information regulations since 1992 but these new regulations are broader in scope, as can be seen in Table 8.1.

Table 8.1   Comparison of the Environmental Information Regulations 1992 and the Environmental Information Regulations 2004, SI 2004/3391

Heading	Main differences
Time limits	Under 1992 the time limit was 2 months, it is now 20 working days.
What is covered	New regulations also cover cost benefit and other economic assumptions, and state of human health and safety.
Who is covered	Now includes bodies who have contracts with the authority.
Advice and assistance	These are new obligations under the 2004 Regulations.
Proactive dissemination	A new requirement.
Transfer of requests	A new obligation.
Up to date, accurate and comparable data	New standards set.
Environmental registers	Not excluded from some of the regulations under the new Regulations.
Data Protection	Provision made in the new Regulations.
Format of information provided	New Regulations require that information is available in the format requested by the requester.
Reasons	More detailed reasons needed.
Exceptions	Grounds for refusing are much narrower.
Appeals and enforcements	Levels of review added.
Information Commissioner	Environmental Information Regulations brought under the Commissioner in line with Freedom of Information Act.
Criminal offences	A new offence added for a person who destroys, defaces or deliberately conceals information requested.

The legislation is a statutory instrument but is secondary to the European Communities Act 1972 (Schedule 2 paragraph 2(2)), which makes European law into British statute. The regulations themselves are, in part, a translation of the original directive. They are very similar to the Freedom of Information Act but have fewer exemptions (the regulations call them exceptions but this is because a different government department drafted them) and they are all subject to the concept of a public interest test. The time limits for responding to environmental information requests are similar to those of freedom of information and so are completely different from those of the Data Protection Act – usually 20 working days rather than 40 calendar days.

There are a few further differences from the Freedom of Information Act, relating to public records and to the way environmental data are handled. These will be examined in Chapter 9.

What can be seen from the above is the importance of making front-line staff aware of the elements of both pieces of legislation and how important it is that Freedom of Information Act and Environmental Information Regulations requests are handled promptly.

8.4   The differences between the Freedom of Information Act 2000 and the Environmental Information Regulations 2004, SI 2004/3391

While the two enactments are similar in intent there are a number of differences between them. Other than the differences relating to exemptions and exceptions, Table 8.2 shows the main differences and how the two enactments compare.

8.5   The section 45 code of practice

Under the Freedom of Information Act there are requirements under sections 45 and 46 for the Secretary of State for Justice, respectively, to issue two codes of practice. The first relates to the discharge of public authority functions and the second to the necessary records management function. The second of these codes, under section 46, will be studied in

Table 8.2   Main differences between the Freedom of Information Act 2000 and the Environmental Information Regulations 2004, SI 2004/3391

Heading	Freedom of Information Act	Environmental Information Regulations
Background	UK law.	Based on European directive and Aarhus Convention.
Scope	Public authorities.	Public authorities plus other bodies dealing with environmental issues of a public nature.
Vexatious or repeated requests	Included as an exemption.	No direct comparison, only manifestly unreasonable. (See Chapter 10)
Proactive dissemination	Not included.	A definite provision of the legislation. (See Chapter 9)
Requests in writing	A requirement.	Can be oral.
Duty to confirm or deny	A requirement.	Not specifically mentioned but implied.
Other prohibitions on disclosure	Not included, in fact other laws take precedence.	Take no effect. Environmental Information Regulations take precedence (regulation 5).
Public interest test	Only applies to some, others are absolute.	None are absolute.
Transfer	Implied under section 16 duty to assist.	Explicit requirement (regulation 10).
Time limits	Can extend for an indefinite period to apply the public interest test.	Can only extend for a period of a further 20 days but does include complex requests.
Appropriate limit	Set for central government (and Scotland) at £600 and for other public authorities £450.	Not applicable.
Charges	Disbursements only under the appropriate limit.	Reasonable charges (*Markinson* v. *Information Commissioner* [2006]).
Information held	Information held by a public authority on behalf of another is not included.	Information held by a public authority is included whether or not it is held on behalf of another authority.

detail in Chapter 15, but the first, under section 45, is examined here as it affects both freedom of information and environmental information.

The section 45 code of practice was presented to Parliament by the Lord Chancellor and is not enforceable in its own right, but failure to follow the code may make an authority accountable to the Information Commissioner. This is especially important if the authority is subject to a Practice Notice, as compliance with the code is one of the main criteria being examined. (A 'Practice Notice' is issued by the Information Commissioner on an authority whose practices in information rights – in the opinion of the Commissioner – need improvement.)

The code declares its main aims as being to:

- facilitate the disclosure of information under the Act by setting out good administrative practice that it is desirable for public authorities to follow when handling requests for information, including, where appropriate, the transfer of a request to a different authority;
- protect the interests of the applicants by setting out standards for the provision of advice which it would be good practice to make available to them and to encourage the development of effective means of complaining about decisions taken under the Act;
- facilitate consideration by public authorities of the interests of third parties who may be affected by any decision to disclose information, by setting standards for consultation; and
- promote consideration by public authorities of the implications for Freedom of Information before agreeing to confidentiality provisions in contracts and accepting information in confidence from a third party more generally.

(The Lord Chancellor's Code of Practice
. . . under Part I of FOIA 2000)

The code is divided into sections, the first dealing with advice and assistance to those making a request. The code places special emphasis on the section 16 duty to assist, reminding public authorities that they should be prepared to give advice and assistance to those making a request as far they can reasonably do so. The code places an obligation on the public authorities to publish advice on how requests for information can be made and reminds the staff of authorities that not everyone will quote the appropriate regulation in their request.

Paragraph 8 highlights how to make a request if the requester cannot write one themselves, suggesting that an individual could be referred to another agency such as the Citizens' Advice bureau for help in making the request. It even suggests that in very exceptional circumstances an authority itself could write out the request, making sure it is then read back to the applicant to ensure that it is accurate.

The code of practice states that an applicant can be asked by the authority, for the purpose of the request, to supply clarifying information, but is not obliged to supply this. Seeking clarification can help the authority to provide more meaningful information to the applicant – and reminds applicants that the request should not be too general.

It is suggested at paragraph 10 of the code that authorities could provide an outline of the different types of information available and give access to detailed catalogues, if these are available, to help the applicant to formulate a request.

The code reminds us that requests made as part of an organized campaign can be cumulative when calculating the appropriate limits (section 12(1) of the Freedom of Information Act). Timeliness in handling requests receives some attention, as this is probably the area where most public authorities are in breach. The time limit for responding is 40 days for most data protection requests and 20 working days for freedom of information and environmental information requests (see Chapter 9.5).

The code describes in detail the duty to transfer a request for information to another authority where the request is not appropriate to the authority that received the request. Where a request is received for information that is held by an authority but that was supplied to it by a third party, the code places an obligation for the third party to be consulted. However, the decision of the authority receiving the request is final.

Public sector contracts were perceived as being difficult even before the Act came into force. The authors of the code give advice that contracts should not describe information as confidential where a confidence does not actually exist and the responsibility for applying the exemption lies with the public authority in the case of any dispute. The provision of a confidentiality clause in a contract can be overridden by the legislation and suppliers should be made aware of this, although the code reminds authorities that there are provisions in the Act to protect any information which is genuinely confidential and can be exempted from requests.

Public authorities are instructed to keep a record of requests where all or part of the information is withheld, although it is necessary to establish what a request is and discount all the 'business as usuals' (everyday requests), as described in Chapter 9.2.

Public authorities are required to have effective complaints procedures which will lead on to the Information Commissioner's own process if necessary. A complaint should not be handled by the same person who is dealing with the request and, the Commissioner has since advised, should be dealt with by a more senior person than the individual who handled the original request.

While issues related to freedom of information requests are covered in the appropriate chapters of this book, the code of practice serves as an easy reference guide.

8.6   Summary

While both enactments mainly relate to access to data they have a major impact on the way in which public authorities must now operate. It is essential that all staff, especially those who deal with the public or receive e-mails and letters from outside their authority, are fully aware of the implications of the legislation and that it has created statutory powers that can be used either by the Information Commissioner or by the courts. Effective staff training on the legislation and staff updates on the latest information and interpretations of the legislation are recommended.

The code of practice does give useful guidance to authorities on how to handle requests, and emphasizes the requirements of section 16, the duty to assist. There is also useful advice on public sector contracts, confidentiality and consultations.

Before we look at the exemptions and exceptions that can be applied, the next chapter will examine the scope of the two enactments and also some of the other sections of the legislation which do not relate to access.

Scope of the Freedom of Information Act 2000 and the Environmental Information Regulations 2004, SI 2004/3391

9.1 Definition of a public authority

Both the Freedom of Information Act 2000 and the Environmental Information Regulations 2004 apply only to the public sector, although the Environmental Information Regulations have a broader definition of the public sector. The Freedom of Information Act lists all authorities that it regards as public authorities in Schedule 1. This is being constantly updated by a steady stream of statutory instruments, at least one a year. The list includes government departments, local authorities, NHS trusts, schools (as separate authorities from the local authority), universities, fire and rescue, police and so on. It also includes private companies wholly owned by a public authority, as defined under section 6 of the Act.

Private companies owned by an authority is interpreted by the Information Commissioner to mean one single authority, so an arm's length management organization (ALMO) for housing set up by a local authority falls under Freedom of Information Act; but an airport run by three local councils does not.

A company partially owned by a public authority is outside the scope of the legislation. Another grouping to which the Act applies, consists of agencies, boards and private companies doing work for a public authority insofar as the work is being carried out for the public sector. This latter group also includes general practitioners and dentists working for the

National Health Service. Even the Information Commissioner is included on the list (this is unique throughout Europe).

The list relates to both freedom of information and environmental information regulations; however, the environmental information regulations list also extends to private companies that carry out public functions affecting the environment.

The actual definition listed at regulation 2(d) states:

(i)   has public responsibilities relating to the environment;

(ii) exercises functions of a public nature relating to the environment or

(iii) provides public services relating to the environment.

(EIR 2004, r. 2(d))

Included here are water companies, electricity and gas suppliers and other similar authorities. The reason for this is that in some countries of Europe these utilities are provided by the public sector. Northern Ireland, for example, has public water suppliers, and in Greece the electricity company collects most utility charges. The Environmental Information Regulations, as has been already stated, are based on European regulations, and so all the European elements have to be taken into account to ensure consistency.

9.2   What is a request?

Under the Freedom of Information Act all data held by a public authority is covered unless one of the exemptions is applicable (see Chapter 10). For this reason it is argued that all requests legally come under the Freedom of Information Act, assuming they are in writing with a name and return address. It is only after the exemptions have been applied that the other two Acts can take effect.

To meet the section 8 requirements it is necessary for the request to be in writing, with a name and return address. It should be noted that a return address can be an e-mail or PO box and the name does not have to be a personal one; indeed, it can be the name of a company or authority. However, if the name is a fictitious one the rights of appeal to the Information Commissioner are waived.

Sufficient information is required to identify the request so, as under the Data Protection Act, it is not sufficient for the requester to state that he wants everything relating to, say, a school, he must be more specific.

It is very important that the actual detail of the request is clarified and not just guessed at – 'I think he might mean this' – otherwise the requester will keep coming back after the information has been supplied. There have been cases before the Information Tribunal where this has been a contributing factor and the Information Commissioner, if he carries out a subsequent inspection, will look into how an authority complied with the duty to give advice and assistance under regulation 9 (or section 16 for the Freedom of Information Act).

However, under the Environmental Information Regulations, it should be noted, requests can be made orally as there is no definition of what constitutes a request, so this widens the scope somewhat. The requester must still give an address to which to respond, and a name. The following would be a typical oral environmental information regulations request:

'My name is Bert Entwhistle of 23 Corporation Street. I walk my dog in the park every day and have noticed the gardeners putting something around the roses. Can you tell me what it is and will it harm my dog?'

In this case the applicant has given both name and return address even though the request was made over the telephone and so it is lawfully a request under the Environmental Information Regulations.

It is not necessary to record every request as coming under the Freedom of Information Act (or Environmental Information Regulations). Those that can be replied to instantly, or at least within a day or so, and where no information has to be removed are classed as business as usual (BAU) and it is only those requests where information has to be removed or where it will take a longer time to respond that must be handled under the legislation.

9.3   Definition of environmental data

Environmental data has a much broader definition than most people might think. It does include the obvious, such as pollution, but also includes planning and built structures. Some authorities have stated that the Environmental Information Regulations do not apply to them. However, by examining the definition given below it will be seen that almost all, if not every authority, needs to take the regulations into account.

If it is not intended to remove any data, provided that a reply can be given within the 20 working days, then which legislation applies to a request does not really make any difference. However, if data is removed or the deadlines cannot be met, the definitions need to be looked at so as to decide which enactment to use.

Regulation 2 states that

environmental information has the same meaning as in Article 2(1) of the
Directive.   (EIR 2004, r. 2)

and goes on to describe what the directive says:

namely any information in written, visual, aural, electronic or any other material
form on:-. . .   (EIR 2004, r. 2)

It then describes the definitions. It will be seen from the above that provided the information is recorded in some form it will come under these regulations. The directive has a series of paragraphs which keep referring to previous paragraphs. Listed below are the paragraphs as they are given in regulation 2 and, after each one, an explanation of how they interact.

(a) the state of the elements of the environment, such as air and atmosphere,
water, soil, land, landscape and natural sites including wet lands, coastal and
marine areas, biological diversity and its components, including genetically
modified organisms, and the interaction among these elements.
                                                                        (EIR 2004, r. 2)

This paragraph, along with paragraph (b) of the same regulation, is the foundation of the definitions and it is to these two that all the other paragraphs relate. These two indicate what are generally accepted as issues affecting the environment, although you will have already spotted that the wording states 'such as' and is therefore not an exhaustive list of the state of the elements.

(b) factors, such as substances, energy, noise, radiation or waste, including radioactive waste, emissions, discharges and other releases into the environment, affecting or likely to affect the elements of the environment referred to in (a).

(EIR 2004, r. 2)

This paragraph also gives some guidance by indicating the types of factors that could be included, but there is already a reference back to paragraph (a). It will be seen that the test is 'Is the information affecting the environment or reporting back on it?' The following example will help to clarify the meaning.

A list of environmental health officers does not to affect the environment and will come under the Freedom of Information Act but a policy on how the environment is protected would be an Environmental Information Regulations request.

---

measures (including administrative measures), such as policies, legislation, plans, programmes, environmental agreements, and activities affecting or likely to affect the elements and factors referred to in (a) and (b) as well as measures or activities designed to protect those elements.   (EIR 2004, r. 2)

It is here that the regulations start to broaden out from what might have been thought of as being purely environmental. Planning is brought in, as the decisions made affect the environment.

(d) reports on the implementation of environmental legislation.

(EIR 2004, r. 2)

This straightforward explanation broadens the scope of the definition still further and now brings in regulations, so that a request for a report on the implementation of the Environmental Information Regulations would need to be handled under EIR.

> (e) cost-benefit and other economic analyses and assumptions used within the
> framework of the measures and activities referred to in (c).
>
> (EIR 2004, r. 2)

So it is not only the final decision which comes under the regulations but also all the build-up to that decision and the supporting evidence.

> (f) the state of human health and safety, including the contamination of the food
> chain, where relevant, conditions of human life, cultural sites and built structures
> inasmuch as they are or may be affected by the state of the elements of the
> environment referred to in (a) or, through those elements, by any matters
> referred to in (b) and (c).
>
> (EIR 2004, r. 2)

This is very wide ranging and brings in a number of other issues. Built structures include roads, railways, trams, airports and the like as they all have an impact on the environment. Some examples are given below of where the data would come under the Environmental Information Regulations.

The new bypass being proposed and the decision-making process behind it fall under these regulations as would repairs to housing stock. Food inspection reports might also be thought of as being administrative measures relating to contamination of the food chain and the Information Tribunal considers, in most cases, that these should be released providing no personal data is involved

---

It will be seen from this that the definition of environmental data is much broader than might at first have been thought. Where a request for information is covered by the Environmental Information Regulations it will be subject to fewer exceptions and restrictions.

If there is any doubt as to which legislation applies, a request must be handled under the legislation which gives the best advantage to the applicant.

9.4   Fees

The regulations for fees differ slightly between the two pieces of legislation. Under the Freedom of Information Act a fee cannot be charged if the cost of finding the information does not exceed the appropriate limit. Currently that limit is set at £600 for central government and Scottish authorities and £450 for all others. This limit is calculated on the basis of £25 an hour. (The Freedom of Information and Data Protection (Appropriate Limit and Fees) Regulations 2004 (SI 2004/3244).) What is not clear is whether this is per hour of searching or per person hour of searching. There is also a question that if a search will exceed the limit for finding the data, which in the case of most authorities is roughly 2½ days of continuous searching or just over 3 days for central government (3.2 days), how could that same data be found if it were needed for the authority's own use. The definition of whether or not information is held will be examined in the next chapter, on exemptions and exceptions.

If the cost of the search will exceed the limit, then there are a number of options. Firstly a request can be refused, but if it is refused, under the duty to assist at section 16 the authority must advise on how the request could be met within the limit. It may be that instead of asking for 10 years of data, five would suffice, bringing the request below the limit. The second option is to tell the requester how much it will cost. This is calculated from day one at the rate of £25 an hour. The third option is to supply what information can be supplied within the limit and say that if more is wanted there will be a fee.

Even if the appropriate limit has not been exceeded, a charge can be made for disbursements, but these should be reasonable. Disbursements include such things as photocopying and postage and should be calculated at cost. There should not be an element of searching time included. In defining 'reasonable' the Information Tribunal has suggested a charge of 10p per A4 page, with larger sizes at actual cost (*Markinson* v. *Information Commission* [2006]).

In this case, which was under Environmental Information Regulations, a local authority allowed Mr Markinson to view a register containing the data he required and then charged him £6 per sheet for a hard copy. The Information

Commissioner considered he was not in a position to decide what was reasonable as far as the charge went and so decided in the Authority's favour. The Authority meanwhile had reduced the charge to 50p but soon put it up again when the decision went its way. The Tribunal found that there were no additional costs involved in finding the documents after the applicant had viewed them and so decided the charge was not reasonable and imposed a charge of 10p per copy.

The charging regime for requests under the Environmental Information Regulations is slightly different. A public authority can charge for making the information available. Regulation 8 states that

> a charge . . . shall not exceed an amount which the public authority is satisfied is a reasonable amount.   (EIR 2004, r. 8)

The test of 'reasonable' can be tried in the courts or the Information Tribunal. Both the Department for the Environment, Food and Rural Affairs (DEFRA) and the Information Commissioner's Office (ICO) recommend that the same charging regime be applied as for the Freedom of Information Act, except that there is no appropriate limit.

The Environmental Information Regulations do state that there can be no charge for access to any public register which comes under its remit. Disbursement charges can also be made under the regulations.

Some authorities place a lower ceiling on charges, as it can cost more to collect the fees than the actual amount requested. This is entirely optional, as the fees are not compulsory.

The information will be sent to the applicant on payment of the fee. The applicant has three months in which to pay after receiving a fees notice. If the fee is not paid in this time, then the information will not be sent and it will be necessary for the requester to make a new request.

9.5   Time limits

Again, both enactments are very similar. Both require that an answer be given to the applicant no later than 20 working days after the date of receipt of the request. This means that the clock starts on the day after the request has been received. Remember that requests under the Environmental Information Regulations can be oral, so it is very important that anyone who may receive a request knows how to handle it as, within this four week period, checks also have to be carried out once the data has been found. The 20 days are classed as working days, Mondays to Fridays, and do not include statutory or bank holidays. They do include the other days an authority may be closed for work, such as the extra days added on to bank holidays by many authorities.

Each piece of legislation has ways in which the time limits can be extended. Under the Environmental Information Regulations, regulation 10, the time can be extended by a further 20 days if it is to handle a complex request or where the public interest test is needed. The time limit cannot be further extended under these regulations.

Under the Freedom of Information Act the time limit can be extended for a reasonable period, but only for the purpose of applying the public interest test. It cannot be extended just because the request is running late. The code of practice under section 45 of the Act suggests that a record should be kept of the extended time and, if it overruns, a note should be made to ensure that it does not happen again. Of course, if it is late, this will be taken into account by the Information Commissioner if he receives a complaint.

In both cases the extended time must be notified to the applicant prior to the expiry of the first period of 20 days.

9.6   Dissemination of environmental information

The Environmental Information Regulations have a specific regulation which refers to the keeping of environmental information. Regulation 4 directs that

4(1)   Subject to paragraph 3

(i.e. the exceptions at regulation 5, which will be listed and considered in Chapter 10), a public authority shall in respect of environmental information that it holds –

(a) progressively make the information available to the public by electronic means which are easily accessible; and

(b) take reasonable steps to organize the information relevant to its functions with a view to the active and systematic dissemination to the public of the information.

(EIR 2004, r. 4)

This means that there is an obligation on public authorities to make environmental information readily available online by keeping it electronically.

9.7   Consultation

The final decision on whether to release information remains with the holding authority. There is, however, a requirement to consult with other interested parties if they were, say, the authors of the document. This could apply to a request to view a successful tender where it was not clear in the contract documents that the tenders would be covered by the Acts. It could equally be the minutes of a multi-agency meeting where items were discussed and it would be necessary to ask the other parties whether they were content with the release of the information.

The other parties cannot appeal the holding authority's decision, other than by taking out an injunction, but their views should be taken into account before making a release. This consultation should be carried out within the 20 days.

9.8   Summary

The first few sections of both enactments define their scope. If requests are to be handled without any removal of data and within the time limit the different scope of the two Acts is not relevant, but otherwise the definitions of each Act are very important, as they determine under which Act a request for information should be handled.

The other sections of the legislation are covered in the following chapters.

Having established in this chapter what constitutes a request, the next stage is to look at the exemptions and exceptions that may apply. These are explained in the next chapter.

10

Application of exemptions and exceptions

10.1   Introduction

Regulation 12 of the Environmental Information Regulations 2004 states that:

> A public authority shall apply a presumption in favour of disclosure.
>
> (EIR 2004, r. 12)

However, there are occasions when some of the data does need to be withheld, and for this purpose the Freedom of Information Act has a list of exemptions in sections 22 to 44 and the Environmental Information Regulations list exemptions under regulation 12. There are a few exemptions elsewhere in the Acts, which will also be listed later in this chapter.

Section 2 of the Freedom of Information Act explains the difference between the two types of exemption that can apply. The first is absolute, indicating that it can be applied without the application of a public interest test. The second is a qualified exemption, to which the public interest test must be applied. This test is explained in Chapter 11. There is a requirement at sections 1(5) and 2(1) to confirm or deny to the requester that information is held, even if the exemption is absolute. The only exception to this is when, by confirming or denying, an answer is given. The example below gives an indication how this might apply.

'How many nuclear missiles does HMS Umbridge have?'
Confirming that the ship has such missiles but not stating how many (defence exemption) reveals a military secret about the vessel. If it is decided not to confirm, then the requester must be told what exemption would apply if the data were held.

When applying any exemption there is a requirement under section 16 to advise and assist. This means that the exemption has to be explained, and also how the public interest applies. This being the case, the following example would answer the request for the military data shown above.

'I am unable to confirm or deny that we have the information you requested. To do so could reveal information covered under section 26 of the Freedom of Information Act 2000 in that it could prejudice the defence of the United Kingdom, and the public interest would not be met in releasing such information.'

Section 17 of the Freedom of Information Act states that if any inform-ation is to be withheld a notice must be given to the requester which:

(a) states the fact [that an exemption applies]
(b) specifies the exemption in question and
(c) states (if that would not otherwise be apparent) why the exemption applies.

(FOIA 2000, s. 17)

The only exception to this is an exemption under section 13, which concerns vexatious or repeated requests (see 10.2.25 below).

Both enactments relate only to information that is held by a public authority. The Environmental Information Regulations have a specific exemption at regulation 12(4)(a), which states:

it does not hold the information when an applicant's request is received

whereas the Freedom of Information Act refers to information held by the public authority.

This leads to a need to define what is meant by 'information held'. There is a clear distinction between information owned or generated by the authority and that held by it. Under this definition it does not matter who was the author of the information, but the fact that it is held is sufficient for it to be released, subject, of course, to the exemptions. There is not quite such a clear distinction between raw data that is held and a request that would require this data to be processed in order to produce an answer. As a rule of thumb it may be regarded that if the information has not been processed in the way a requester wishes, and does not need such processing for the operation of the service it supports, then there is no requirement to generate the additional information. The following example may make this clearer.

Information on the number of parking fines on High Street over the past twelve months is clearly held and needed for the operation of the service. A request for the number of parking fines on High Street where the cars in question were of French manufacture would be difficult to answer. The information is held in its raw state and is only used if there is a query on the fine to establish if it was the correct vehicle, but it is not stored on the database as it is not required as part of the normal operation of the service. It would be necessary to examine each ticket and create a list especially for the requester. If the requested information was stored on the database and could be retrieved with little effort, then it should be released, if to do so would not take longer than the prescribed limit. The next question concerns whether the information held relates to the request. If it does not, the request can be refused. To be helpful, the authority could give the overall total of fines on the street.

When applying exemptions it is rarely possible to apply them in a blanket fashion. For example, just because a document says 'DRAFT' this does not mean that it will be exempt. This will be examined later in this chapter (see 10.3.6).

The main exemptions listed in section 10.2 are under the Freedom of Information Act. Although the exceptions of the Environmental Information Regulations are explained later in this chapter, they are listed alongside the exemptions so that it can be seen how the two enactments interact.

10.2 Exemptions under the Freedom of Information Act

10.2.1 Section 21 Information accessible to the applicant by other means

21(1) Information which is reasonably accessible to the applicant otherwise than under section 1 is exempt information. (FOIA 2000, s. 21(1))

Section 1 is a request for information. Section 21 is absolute and so the public interest test does not apply. The section states that if information is available without making a request then the Freedom of Information Act does not apply.

The equivalent environmental information regulation (r. 6) states that

the information is already publicly available and easily accessible to the applicant in another form or format. (EIR 2004, r. 6)

Information that is already listed in a publication scheme would be covered by this section (see Chapter 12). However, the phrase 'reasonably accessible' will have been noticed. This does not mean that a charge cannot be made for supplying the information, especially if this is indicated in the publication scheme and provided that any charge is reasonable.

If the information is accessible elsewhere, then the requester should expect to be directed to it. However, the authority should always check that the other organization actually has the information and can supply it. This is particularly important if the other organization is not covered by the Freedom of Information Act or the Environmental Information Regulations (for example, in a request about the use of vehicles by a bus company not wholly owned by a public authority). The code of practice issued by the Secretary of State for Constitutional Affairs under section 45 emphasizes the duty under section 16 to assist, and that there is a duty to pass the request on to another authority if this is known.

If the information is available on a website and is not very extensive it may well be worth providing it to the requester anyway, provided that no charge is made for the information. Otherwise, the URL for the information should be provided. It is not very helpful to the requester to make them reapply for information just because it is available elsewhere in the same authority.

10.2.2 Section 22 Information intended for future publication

The definition of this exemption is quite wide:

(a) the information is held by the public authority with a view to its publication, by the authority or by any other person, at some future date (whether determined or not)

(b) the information was already held with a view to such publication at the time the request was made and

(c) it is reasonable in all circumstances that the information should be withheld from disclosure until the date referred to in paragraph (a).

(FOIA 2000, s. 22)

The exception is very similar under Environmental Information Regulations (r. 12(4)(d)):

The request relates to material which is still in the course of completion, to unfinished documents or to incomplete data.   (EIR 2004, r. 12(4)(d))

In the Scottish Act this exception is more restrictive in that the items have to be published within three months, but for the rest of the UK no date is given. In fact paragraph (a) states that there does not have to be a date or time in mind, although the code of practice does state that the requester should be given an idea as to when they may get the information and best practice dictates that the authority should consider making a note to send the information out when it is published.

This exemption is qualified, and even paragraph (c) states that a test of reasonableness should be applied in withholding the information.

The test that should be applied to this type of data would probably be: is there a probability of change in the data or would an early release give a company or individual an unfair advantage? The public interest test should also be applied. The authority may well consider that the information is of such importance that it should be released, but that details which are likely to change should be highlighted (e.g. the closure of a school, or a new road).

10.2.3 Section 23 Information supplied by or relating to bodies dealing with security matters

This section only applies to those authorities listed at section 23(3) of the Act, although it does include any part of the armed forces helping out the government communications headquarters.

This section requires a certificate signed by the Secretary of State stating that the data comes under section 23 before the exemption can be applied. A similar restriction does not apply under the Environmental Information Regulations, although it is always advisable to follow the same rules.

The equivalent exception in the Environmental Information Regulations is r. 12(5)(a).

This is an absolute exemption, so the public interest test will not be applied.

10.2.4 Section 24 National security

This section covers information that does not fall under section 23 but is still required for safeguarding national security. A signed certificate is required from the Secretary of State, but this is only a qualified exemption, so a public interest test must be applied before the information is exempted. The Environmental Information Regulations do not require a certificate, but it is worth dealing with similar information under each enactment in the same way (r. 2(5)(a)).

10.2.5 Section 25 Certificates

This section describes a certificate as being a document or a certified true copy of a document issued under sections 23 or 24 of this Act. A certified true copy also has to be declared as such by the Secretary of State.

This power for the issue of certificates can only be given to Ministers of the Crown who are members of the Cabinet or the Attorney General, the Advocate General for Scotland or the Attorney General for Northern Ireland and only relates to defence issues, so it does not affect most government departments and non-governmental authorities.

10.2.6 Section 26 Defence

(1) Information is exempt information if its disclosure under this Act would, or would be likely to, prejudice –

(a) The defence of the British Islands or of any colony, or

(b) the capacity, effectiveness or security of any relevant forces.

(FOIA 2000, s. 26)

A relevant force is the armed forces or any part of them. It is interesting to note that this is not an absolute exemption but is subject to a test of public interest. Obviously this exemption will not apply to most authorities but only to the relevant government departments.

The equivalent exception in the Environmental Information Regulations is r. 12(5)(a).

10.2.7 Section 27 International relations

International relations relate to the United Kingdom as a state, not to individual areas of the country:

(1) Information is exempt information if its disclosure under this Act would, or would be likely to, prejudice –

(a) relations between the United Kingdom and any other State,

(b) relations between the United Kingdom and any international authority or international court,

(c) the interests of the United Kingdom abroad or

(d the promotion or protection by the United Kingdom of its interests abroad.

(2) Information is also exempt if it is confidential information obtained from a State other than the United Kingdom or from an international authority or international court.

(FOIA 2000 s. 27)

This makes the definition of international relations wider than just between countries as it brings in international authorities such as the Red Cross and the various European and international courts. This exemption is also subject to the public interest test at the time of the request.

The equivalent exception in the Environmental Information Regulations is:

(a) international relations, defence, national security or public safety.

(EIR 2004, r. 12(5)(a))

10.2.8 Section 28 Relations within the United Kingdom

This only applies where release of information would prejudice relations between the administration of the United Kingdom (government) and any other administration. The section describes these administrations as:

(a) the government of the United Kingdom

(b) the Scottish Administration

(c) the Executive Committee of the Northern Ireland Assembly and

(d) the National Assembly for Wales.

(FOIA 2000, s. 28)

This exemption only, therefore, affects those authorities covered by the list and is subject to the public interest. The definition of 'Government of the United Kingdom' also includes any government agencies. The nearest equivalent exception under Environmental Information Regulations is that of internal communications (regulation 12(4)(e)), which also includes information between government agencies.

10.2.9 Section 29 The economy

There is no equivalent exception under the Environmental Information Regulations. This again is an exemption which relates to central government only. The section itself does refer to any part of the United Kingdom but does also refer to administrations as described in section 28.

(1) Information is exempt if its disclosure under the Act would, or be likely to, prejudice

(a) the economic interests of the United Kingdom or any part of the United Kingdom or

(b) the financial interests of any administration of the United Kingdom.

(FOIA 2000, s. 29)

This section is subject to the public interest test.

10.2.10 Section 30 Investigations and proceedings conducted by public authorities

These paragraphs apply across the whole of the public sector and relate to:

(1) (a) any investigation which the public authority has a duty to conduct with a view to it being ascertained –

(i)   whether a person should be charged with an offence, or

(ii) whether a person charged with an offence is guilty of it,

(b) any investigation which is conducted by the authority and in the circumstances may lead to a decision by the authority to institute criminal proceedings which the authority has the power to conduct, or

(c) any criminal proceedings which the authority has power to conduct.

Information held by a public authority is exempt information if:

(2) (a) it was obtained or recorded by the authority for the purposes of its functions relating to –

(i)   investigations falling within subsections (1)(a) or (b),

(ii) criminal proceedings which the authority has the power to conduct,

(iii) investigations . . . which are conducted by the authority for purposes of [law enforcement] or by virtue of powers conferred by or under any enactment, or

(iv) civil proceedings which are brought by or on behalf of the authority and arise out of such investigations, and

(b) it relates to the obtaining of information from confidential sources.

(FOIA 2000, s. 30)

There is a great deal of emphasis on criminal matters, although the penultimate paragraph does introduce civil proceedings. This means that investigations into such matters as antisocial behaviour (ASB) which can be either criminal or civil are covered. It be should noted, however, that this all relates to the authority which has the powers to carry out the investigation. Where there are joint operations, such as those with the Department for Work and Pensions (DWP), this exemption can only be used by the authority with the power to investigate and not by its partner authority. The question to ask is: 'Who brings about any prosecution?' The answer will identify the authority that may apply this exemption. If an authority is not the investigating authority, it should refer to the exemption under section 31.

Criminal proceedings include courts martial and charges under the Army Act 1955, the Air Force Act 1955 or the Naval Discipline Act 1957. The public interest test applies to this section.

The equivalent exception in the Environmental Information Regulations is r. 12(5)(b).

10.2.11 Section 31 Law Enforcement

This section lists the subjects that are not covered by section 30.

31(1) Information which is not exempt information by virtue of section 30 [Investigations] is exempt information if its disclosure under this Act would, or would be likely to, prejudice –

(a) the prevention or detection of crime,

(b) the apprehension or prosecution of offenders,

(c) the administration of justice,

(d) the assessment or collection of any tax or duty or of any imposition of a similar nature,

(e) the operation of the immigration controls,

(f) the maintenance of security and good order in prisons . . .,

(g) the exercise by any public authority of its functions for any of the purposes specified in subsection 2,

(h) any civil proceedings which are brought by or on behalf of a public authority . . . by virtue of any enactment . . . .

(2)(a) the purpose of ascertaining whether any person has failed to comply with the law,

(b) the purpose of ascertaining whether any person is responsible for any conduct which is improper,

(c) the purpose of ascertaining whether circumstances which would justify regulatory action in pursuance of any enactment . . . ,

(d) the purpose of ascertaining a person's fitness or competence in relation to the management of bodies corporate or in relation to any profession or other activity which he is or seeks to become authorised to carry out,

(e) the purpose of ascertaining the cause of an accident,

(f) the purpose of protecting the property of charities from loss or misapplication,

(g) the purpose of recovering the property of charities from loss or misapplication,

(h) the purpose of recovering the property of charities,

(i) the purpose of securing the health, safety and welfare of persons at work and,

(j) the purpose of protecting persons, other than persons at work, against risk to health or safety arising out of or in connection with the actions of persons at work.

(FOIA 2000, s. 31)

Although this section is headed 'law enforcement' a great many other areas are covered, ranging from crime detection to improper conduct. The section is subject to the public interest test although the duty to confirm or deny will only apply if it would not be likely to prejudice any of the investigations that are listed. In this section it will have been noticed that the information does not have to be held by the investigating authority, which gives this section a great deal of scope for application.

The equivalent regulation in the Environmental Information Regulations is r. 12(5)(b).

10.2.12 Section 32 Court records, etc.

Because this section of the Freedom of Information Act is absolute, there is no requirement to apply the public interest test. The nearest equivalent in Environmental Information Regulations is regulation 12(5)(b), which is subject to a public interest test. However, there would be a duty to consult with the court and it would not be wise to proceed against the court's view.

Court records are specified as being:

(a) Any document filed with, or otherwise placed in the custody of, a court for the purposes of proceedings . . .

(b) Any document served upon, or by, a public authority for the purposes of proceedings . . .

(c) Any document created by –
   (i) a court or
   (ii) a member of the administrative staff of a court.

(FOIA 2000, s. 32)

Courts are also defined as including statutory inquiries, tribunals and arbitration. Just because a document has been presented in court does not mean that it is a court record. The papers are those prepared for court which it is normal to obtain consent from the court to release. The duty to confirm or deny does not apply to this section.

The equivalent regulation in the Environmental Information Regulations is r. 12(5)(b) and 3(3).

10.2.13 Section 33 Audit functions

This section does not relate to a public authority's own internal audit, as it states that it is in relation to the audit of accounts of other public authorities. The public authorities that may apply this exemption are those whose function it is to carry out audits on others. The duty to confirm or deny does not apply if it would prejudice any investigation or audit being carried out, although the public interest test does apply because this section is only a qualified exemption.

The equivalent regulation in the Environmental Information Regulations is r. 12(5)(b).

10.2.14 Section 34 Parliamentary privilege

This is an absolute exemption and is required to avoid an infringement of the privileges of either House of Parliament. The duty to confirm or deny does not apply if it would breach those privileges, although a certificate is required if this exemption is applied. The certificate has to be signed by the Speaker of the House in relation to the House of Commons and the Clerk of the Parliament where the House of Lords is concerned.

There are no equivalent regulations in the Environmental Information Regulations.

10.2.15 Section 35 Function of government policy, etc.

The Act explains this quite clearly:

35(1) Information held by a government department or by the National Assembly of Wales is exempt information if it relates to –

(a) the formulation or development of government policy

(b) Ministerial communications

(c) the provision of advice by any of the Law officers or any request for the provision of such advice or

(d) the operation of any Ministerial private office.

(FOIA 2000, s. 35)

The nearest equivalent exemption in the Environmental Information Regulations is that for the disclosure of internal communications, r. 12(4)(e).

This particular exemption under the Freedom of Information Act also includes the Executive Committee of the Northern Ireland Assembly and the National Assembly for Wales. It relates only to information held by government departments. If the authority being requested for the information is not a government department, this exemption does not apply even to Ministerial communications.

Once the policy has been formulated any statistical information used to provide background for that policy cannot use this exemption. The exemption is not absolute, so the public interest test applies.

10.2.16 Section 36 Prejudice to the effective conduct of public affairs

This section is unique in the operation of exemptions in that it is in two separate parts and the exemption cannot be applied by the normal means. The nearest exception in Environmental Information Regulations is that for the disclosure of internal communications, which covers opinions generated within a public authority (r. 12(4)(e)). The first part of this section is only an absolute exemption insofar as it relates to the Houses of Parliament.

The wording of the rest of the section is:

(2) Information to which this section applies is exempt information if, in the reasonable opinion of a qualified person, disclosure of the information under this Act –

(a) would, or would be likely to, prejudice –

(i) the maintenance of the convention of the collective responsibility of Ministers of the Crown, or

(ii) the work of the Executive Committee of the Northern Ireland Assembly or

(iii) the work of the executive committee of the National Assembly for Wales.

(FOIA 2000, s. 36)

Obviously these paragraphs relate only to central government and those assemblies mentioned. The next part of the section relates to the rest of the public sector as well:

(b) would, or would likely to inhibit –
  (i) the free and frank provision of advice or
  (ii) the free and frank exchange of views for the purposes of deliberation or
     would otherwise prejudice, or would be likely otherwise to prejudice, the
     effective conduct of public affairs.

(FOIA 2000, s. 36)

Both the first paragraph and the paragraph at section 36(3), which refers to the application of the duty to confirm or deny, make reference to a qualified person. The exemption can only be applied by a qualified person who will also apply the public interest test.

Section 36(5) gives a list of who is regarded as a qualified person. The list can be better qualified by an instruction from the Secretary of State for Constitutional Affairs under section 36(5)(o)(iii), which he did in January 2005, and which is now available on the Ministry of Justice website (www. justice.gov.uk). The easiest way to review this section is through Table 10.1 (overleaf).

In each case the authorizing officer is a very senior officer in the authority. Problems occur with authorities such as arm's length management organizations (ALMO), which currently would have to apply to the Minister at the Department for Communities and Local Government for authority to use this exemption.

If the information relates to either House of Parliament, all that is needed is a certificate of exemption.

10.2.17 Section 37 Communications with Her Majesty etc. and honours

As this exemption is not absolute it is necessary to apply the public interest test. The wording of the section explains the full scope:

37(1) Information is exempt information if it relates to –
     (a) communications with Her Majesty, with other members of the Royal
        Family or with the Royal Household or
     (b) the conferring by the Crown of any honour or dignity.

(FOIA 2000, s. 37)

Table 10.1 Qualified persons under section 36(5) of the Freedom of Information Act 2000

Public Authority	Authority	Note
Government department in the charge of a Minister of the Crown	Minister of the Crown	
Northern Ireland Department	Northern Ireland Minister in charge of the department	
Other government department	Commissioner or other person in charge	
House of Commons	Speaker of that House	
House of Lords	Clerk of the Parliament	
Northern Ireland Assembly	Presiding Officer	
National Assembly for Wales	Assembly First Secretary	
Welsh public authority	Any officer or employee of the authority authorised by the Assembly First Secretary	The authority's monitoring officer or, in his absence, the Chief Executive
National Audit Office (and the National Audit office for Northern Ireland or Wales)	Comptroller and Auditor General (for Ireland or Wales)	
Other Northern Ireland public authorities	Officer or employee authorised by the First Minister or Deputy First Minister in Northern Ireland	The authority's monitoring officer or, in his absence, the Chief Executive
Greater London Authority	Mayor of London	
Functional body within the meaning of the Greater London Authority Act 1999	Chairman of that authority	
Other public authority	1) A Minister of the Crown 2) A public authority authorised by a Minister of the Crown 3) An officer or employee of the public authority who is authorised by a Minister of the Crown	The authority's monitoring officer or, in his absence, the Chief Executive. For those that do not have such an officer, it is the Minister who must give approval

The exemption applies to correspondence both to and from the Royal Family.

There are no equivalent regulations in the Environmental Information Regulations.

10.2.18 Section 38 Health and safety

Section 38 requires the public interest test to be applied after the exemption has been identified:

38(1) Information is exempt information if its disclosure under this Act would or
    would be likely to –
    (a) endanger the physical or mental health of any individual or
    (b) endanger the safety of any individual.

(FOIA 2000, s. 38)

The wording of the Act is, in this case, quite clear in that any information
that could endanger the health or safety of anyone can be exempt.

The equivalent regulation in the Environmental Information Regulations is r. 12(5)(a).

10.2.19 Section 39 Environmental information

As was seen earlier, any request received by a public authority is
technically a request under the Freedom of Information Act. This is the
first of two sections which identify those requests that fall under one of
the other two enactments in the information rights trilogy.

Section 74 of the Act permits the Secretary of State to create regulations
based on the Aarhus Convention. These we now know as the Environmental Information Regulations 2004.

Section 39 states that if the information comes under the Environmental
Information Regulations 2004, then these regulations should be used. The
exemption is not absolute as all exceptions under the Environmental
Information Regulations 2004 are subject to the public interest test.

10.2.20 Section 40 Personal information

This exemption is absolute and the public interest test does not apply. The
rule relating to this exemption is that if the data falls under the definition
of personal data (see Chapter 3), then this exemption will apply and the
Data Protection Act 1998 should be used.

Great care must be taken in the definition of personal data. Just because
a name is mentioned the information will not necessarily come under the
Data Protection Act. The definitions given in the Act need to be consulted for clarification, as should any relevant case law, such as *Durant* v.

FSA [2003], which was explained in Chapter 3.

Other tests include: does the information state anything about a named individual or about an official or post? For guidance on this it will be necessary to look at the decision of the Information Commissioner against Corby Borough Council in 2005 (Decision Notice FS50062124).

A request was made of Corby Borough Council for information on the salary of an officer who was in a somewhat controversial post. Corby exempted the information under section 40 because it was, in its opinion, personal data. The requester appealed to the ICO, who disagreed with this view. The main issue is: does the information tell the requester about the officer or the post? A salary scale or a grade relates to the post, but where an individual appears on that scale could well be personal. Also, there is a lesser expectation of privacy regarding the details of some post holders than of others.

There are also more positive examples, such as the one given next.

The Rural Support Agency, which gives out grants to farmers, was asked for the amounts of grants from Europe given to farms over a certain value, listed by farm. It considered applying section 40; however, it was decided that the grant was given to the farm (a business) and not the farmer. It would be possible, by walking around the outside of a farm, to work out how much grant each farm would get, if one knew the rates of grant, so commercial confidentiality could not be claimed (section 43).

The equivalent exception in the Environmental Information Regulations is r. 13.

10.2.21 Section 41 Information provided in confidence

This exemption under the Freedom of Information Act is absolute so there is no need to apply the public interest test. The wording of the exemption states the conditions that must be applied:

(b) the disclosure of the information . . . by the public authority holding it would constitute a breach of confidence actionable by that or any other person.

(FOIA 2000, s. 41)

The key word in this section is 'actionable'. There has to be a probability of legal action against the authority, and also a probability of that action being successful. This means that the word 'confidential' at the head of a document is not sufficient grounds for exemption. The information in question must be supplied from outside the authority. If it were generated by the authority itself, it could not take action against itself for a breach of confidence. If the information is supplied from outside, then, for the breach of confidentiality to be actionable, there has to be actual damage or potential damage to the originator. If this is the case, it is possible that this exemption should be applied. However, confusion can arise between this exemption and that under section 43, commercial interest (see below).

The exception under the Environmental Information Regulations (r. 12(5)(d)) is described as:

(d) the confidentiality of the proceedings of that or any other public authority where such confidentiality is provided by law.

(EIR 2004, r. 12(5)(d))

This is very similar to the exemption at section 41 of the Freedom of Information Act except that, as with all other exceptions (excepting regulation 13, personal data) it is subject to the public interest test.

10.2.22 Section 42 Legal professional privilege

The exception under section 42 concerns:

(1) Information in respect of which a claim to legal privilege . . . could be maintained in legal proceedings.

(FOIA 2000, s. 42)

This section is subject to the public interest test and legal privilege itself is usually a common law right so it is from common law that a definition of legal privilege must be sought.

Just because a letter has been written by a solicitor it does not constitute legal privilege. For example, a note saying, 'Could we meet at 3.00 on Tuesday' does not constitute legal privilege, as it does not affect litigation. However, if a comment is legal advice or opinion it would certainly come under this definition. When, in the next chapter, the definition of the public interest test is examined you will note that an exemption has first to be identified before the test can be applied, so even where there is legal privilege the public interest test may still dictate release.

Lawyers argue that all correspondence from them is covered by this exemption because it is in the public interest to maintain the confidentiality between the client and the lawyer. It is up to individual authorities whether or not they agree; however, the objective of the legislation is to secure the release of information and this should always be the primary consideration. A good test is to assess the potential damage to the authority or to the case in question if the information is released.

The exception that falls nearest to this in the Environmental Information Regulations is that of the disclosure of internal communications (r. 12(4)(e)) or

> the ability of a public authority to conduct an inquiry of a criminal or disciplinary nature.   (EIR 2004, 12 (5)(b))

10.2.23 Section 43 Commercial interest

This section does not need the test of legal action, unlike the exemption at section 41. There are two categories under this exemption:

> 43 (1) Information is exempt information if it constitutes a trade secret.
>
> (2) Information is exempt information if its disclosure under this Act would, or would be likely to, prejudice the commercial interest of any person (including the public authority holding it).
>
> (FOIA 2000, s. 43)

This is probably the exemption most frequently applied by public authorities as it is relatively easy to argue that a requester could be in a better position than a competitor if he received the information. The best test is to assess the potential damage either to the authority or to the originating organization if this information were released. Obviously this argument would not hold if a contract still had many years to run, as no advantage can be achieved for retendering. It is also possible that the whole of a contract is not covered by the exemption. Contract figures are usually available in the authority's annual accounts and so they are already available for inspection part of the year without recourse to the Freedom of Information Act. Day work rates, however, or production methods could be covered as to release these could prejudice the contractor's ability to submit further tenders and could give competitors an unfair advantage. Further guidance on this exemption is given at paragraph 10.3.13 of this chapter.

This exemption is subject to the public interest test. The equivalent regulations in the Environmental Information Regulations are rs. 12(5)(c) and 12(5)(e).

10.2.24 Section 44 Prohibitions on disclosure

In this section one of three conditions must be met:

(a) is prohibited under any enactment

(b) is incompatible with any Community obligation or

(c) would constitute or be punishable as a contempt of court.

(FOIA 2000, s. 44)

Here there is a big difference between the Freedom of Information Act and the Environmental Information Regulations. Under the Freedom of Information Act if another enactment says that something cannot be released, then that overrides the Freedom of Information Act. A regularly used example is the Enterprise Act 2002, which relates to investigations into traders and companies. (In Scotland this is not the case.) In replies using this exemption the actual legislation that prohibits sharing must always be quoted.

However, the Environmental Information Regulations state at regulation 5(6):

Any enactment or rule of law that would prevent the disclosure of information in accordance with these regulations shall not apply.

So the Enterprise Act and similar legislation cannot prohibit the release of environmental data (for a definition see Chapter 9.3).

10.2.25 Section 14 Vexatious or repeated requests

This exemption is not part of the main group of exemptions from sections 21 to 44 and should only apply as a last resort.

Guidance from the Information Commissioner suggests that a repeated request is not only a request for the same or similar information from one person but could also come from a group of individuals. Therefore an action group cannot keep asking for the same information by using different members in the hope of trying to catch an authority out at some point. There are two considerations to be borne in mind. First, when was the last time a request was made? If it was within 60 days the request would definitely be repeated. And second, what has changed in the data since it was last sent out? If nothing has changed, then the applicant can be told so; if there has been a change only the changed data needs to be supplied.

Occasionally a request may be received from someone who has been upset by an authority. It is possible, for example, that he keeps getting a parking fine. Such a person occasionally puts in multiple requests surrounding, in this case, parking. A request will be answered the first time it is received, but the purpose of the multiple requests could well be not to find out information but to cause a nuisance and disrupt the working of the office. If this is perceived to be the case, then this exemption can be applied. There is no need to tell the requester that he is regarded as vexatious, which could cause even more trouble, although the authority may want to tell him that it has already answered his questions and will not answer any more.

In dealing with vexatious or repeated requests, care should be taken not to overlook any request relating to a genuinely different subject, as it is only those that are repeated that can claim this exemption. An Information Commissioner's Decision Notice against Birmingham City Council in 2006 directed that most requests from an individual were vexatious, but that one or two required answers.

The exception under the Environmental Information Regulations (r. 12(4)(b)) is somewhat wider and would apply if the effort in obtaining the information were not proportionate to the information provided, rather like the appropriate limit under section 13 of the Freedom of Information Act. You will also recall that there is a similar exemption under the Data Protection Act (see paragraph 6.2.5, Chapter 6).

10.2.26 Other exemptions

There is a requirement on the applicant to provide a name and address and also to give a reasonable explanation of the information requested. If these details are not supplied, the request will not be answered. This exemption was explained earlier in Chapter 9.2 and 9.4. Similarly there is no requirement to supply the requested information if the appropriate fee has not been paid within the time limit (3 months) (section 9). These are both explained in Chapter 9.

10.3   Exceptions under the Environmental Information Regulations

While looking at the various Freedom of Information Act exemptions above, the equivalent Environmental Information Regulations exception has been referred to. However, there are additional exceptions which relate purely to the Environmental Information Regulations and some of those listed earlier may not match exactly with the definitions of the Freedom of Information Act. There are only 14 exceptions that may apply under the Environmental Information Regulations, most of them listed under regulation 12(4) and (5). All the exceptions under this particular regulation are subject to the public interest test and there is a statutory duty under this regulation (12(3)) to apply a presumption in favour of disclosure.   (EIR 2004, r. 12(3))

Information relating to emissions is not exempt even though it may appear to fall under one of the exceptions listed below. This relates not only to the raw data on emissions, but is wider in that it also includes any data that may relate to emissions.

10.3.1 Regulation 12(3) Personal data

This exception is the only one under regulation 12 that is not subject to the public interest test. The exception itself refers to regulation 13, which has the same meaning as the exception under section 40 of the Freedom of Information Act, described above at paragraph 10.2.20. If the information is defined as personal data under the Data Protection Act then it should not be disclosed under this regulation. This does not mean that third party data should always be withheld, and the various tests suggested in Chapter 3, and paragraph 10.2.20 of this chapter should be applied.

10.3.2 Regulation 6 Information publicly available

This regulation does not just refer to an authority's publication scheme (see Chapter 12), although if the information is listed in the scheme there is an obvious advantage, because it can be proved that the information is available to the public elsewhere. There is a duty to advise the requester of where the information can be obtained (regulation 9, Duty to give advice and assist) and, of course, if it is easy to supply the required information, this should be done.

   If the information is available from outside the authority it should check with the appropriate organization to ensure that the data can be obtained, before redirecting the requester. This is a similar duty to that under the Freedom of Information Act.

   Information held as part of a public register has to be made available, under regulation 6, and must be disclosed without any fee (regulation 8).

10.3.3 Regulation 12(4)(a) Information not held

As with the Freedom of Information Act, there is no requirement to actually generate information, although there is a requirement to make environmental information progressively available to the public by electronic means, from the date of the order, December 2004 (Regulation 4).

The same rules therefore apply as were explained above in paragraph 10.1. Even if the raw data is held, if it is not required for operational use by the authority in the form requested, then it does not have to be provided unless

> it is reasonable for it [the public authority] to make the information available in another form or format. (EIR 2004, r. 6)

Therefore, if the information can easily be supplied from a database, for example, it must be supplied; but if this is not possible there is no requirement to provide the data.

10.3.4 Regulation 12(4)(b) Request manifestly unreasonable

This regulation has a much wider definition than the equivalent 'vexatious' exemption under the Freedom of Information Act.

Not only does it cover repeated or vexation requests but it could also cover requests where it would take an unreasonable amount of time to locate the information, in the same way as the appropriate limit under the Freedom of Information Act. However, this does not mean that, just because an authority has poor records management and will therefore take a long time to find the information, the requester must be at a disadvantage. There is still a requirement under the code of practice issued by the Lord Chancellor to improve records management to ensure this does not happen (see Chapter 15).

10.3.5 Regulation 12(4)(c) Request is too general

If a request is too general and an authority cannot actually identify what information the requester wants it must first go back to them and ask for clarification. This is an actual requirement of the regulation. If the requester still keeps asking for everything or does not really know what they want then this exception can be applied.

The exception actually makes it a requirement that the regulation 9 duty is applied before that of 12(4)(c):

> The request for information is formulated in too general a manner and the public authority has complied with regulation 9.   (EIR 2004, r. 9)

10.3.6 Regulation 12(4)(d) Draft documents

This regulation states:

> relates to material which is still in the course of completion, to unfinished documents or incomplete data.   (EIR 2004, r. 12(4))

Again, as in the Freedom of Information Act, this does not mean that the word 'draft' exempts the document. If it is unfinished, an authority is under a duty to state when it expects it to be finished – this is part of the duty to assist under regulation 9. It is also a requirement of regulation 14(4) that, if this exemption is applied, then

> the authority shall also specify, if known to the public authority, the name of any other public authority preparing the information and the estimated time in which the information will be finished or completed.   (EIR 2004, r. 14(4))

A document that will never be finished can hardly be regarded as a draft. It is argued by some authors that earlier drafts do not fall under this exception, although this is not a view held by everyone. It should also be remembered that there is the public interest test to be applied, and this may override any opinion given to withhold the draft.

10.3.7 Regulation 12(4)(e) Internal communications

This exception sounds as though it could be applied to every memo or e-mail passed between officers. This is not the case (the obligation is to release as much information as possible). The purpose of this regulation is to allow internal discussion on a proposal or policy to proceed without fear that every single thought will be in the public domain, or, as Phil Michaels of Friends of the Earth puts it, to 'allow an authority to think in private'.

If officers felt that every idea and proposal would be made public, they would not be free and open in their discussions, so this regulation helps to promote the free and frank debate (as the Freedom of Information Act states) between officers.

10.3.8 Regulation 12(5) Adversely affect

Regulation 5 groups a number of exceptions together and applies the proviso that information may only be withheld where it would adversely affect the subject of the exception. An authority must, therefore, be able to prove the probability of adverse effect. This must be quite definite, as a possibility could arise in many cases but, although possible, the effect might never happen. There would thus have to be a strong probability before these exceptions were applied, and even then there is the public interest test to follow.

10.3.9 Regulation 12(5)(a) International relations, defence, national security or public safety

Under this exception there is no need to confirm or deny that the information is held or even exists (regulation 12(6), which allows an authority to neither confirm nor deny that the information exists). Public safety could apply where releasing the information would create unnecessary suffering and worry to members of the public, although again it should be remembered that there may well be a public interest in overriding this.

10.3.10 Regulation 12(5)(b) Justice and crime

This is quite a long exception.

The course of justice, the ability of a person to receive a fair trial or the ability of a public authority to conduct an inquiry of a criminal or disciplinary nature.

(EIR 2004, r. 12(5))

This is more restrictive than the equivalent exemption under the Freedom of Information Act. The first test is that the release of the data would prejudice these issues, not just that there is a chance that it may. The exception applies to the courts and fair trial, with obvious reference to the Human Rights Act 1998. It also refers to investigations by a public authority into criminal matters. This is not just for police use (fly tipping, for example, is now a criminal offence) but it does exclude civil disorder issues unless there is the probability of criminal action. Disciplinary nature includes all those issues described under the Freedom of Information Act for military matters as well as internal procedures.

10.3.11 Regulation 12(5)(c) Intellectual property rights

This includes all copyright protected material, patented designs and trade secrets. It is not the intention of either enactment to override and prejudice an individual's or even an organization's rights to protection under copyright laws, although copyright law does not prohibit disclosure under either of the two enactments – only further use of the information. It must be considered whether there would be a breach of intellectual property rights if it was known that the requester intended to reuse the data, and consideration should be given to issuing a licence or restriction under the Re-use of Public Sector Information Regulations 2005 (Chapter 16).

10.3.12 Regulation 12(5)(d) Confidentiality of proceedings

This regulation only permits the exception for confidentiality of proceedings where there is a legal requirement. If this is the case it would be reasonable to expect that the actual law is quoted. This does not apply to any other legal requirement of confidentiality and mainly relates to work with the courts. For those in local government, the revised section 12A exemption as amended in 2005 is not relevant and can be overridden by Freedom of Information and Environmental Information laws.

10.3.13 Regulation 12(5)(e) Commercially confidential

There has to be a legal requirement to prove confidentiality, although the reason could be that there is the probability of legal action and (as in the Freedom of Information Act), there is a strong chance of the action being successful. The exception also relates to industrial information, and so could apply to trade secrets. As the public interest test must be applied this could well override an exception being applied.

If this exemption is to be considered then it would normally need to be shown that the protected person would suffer actual commercial or competitive disadvantage if the information were to be released.

In relation to this exception, case law does give some guidance, *Secretary of State for the Environment, Transport and the Regions and Midland Expressway Ltd v. Alliance Against the Birmingham Northern Relief Road and Others* [1999], which was a challenge under the old 1992 Regulations.

The court decided that: (a) any reference to confidentiality must mean specific information which a company needs to keep confidential in order to protect its competitive position, (b) what is or is not confidential is objective, (c) not all of a particular contract can be regarded as confidential, and (d) confidentiality would depend upon the time when a request was made.

The Department for Environment, Food and Rural Affairs (DEFRA) suggests that confidentiality clauses should be avoided if possible. If there are any such clauses these regulations may override them, and any legal obligations cannot be overruled by a contract.

10.3.14 Regulation 12(5)(f) Information supplied in confidence

This exception relates to the release of information that would adversely affect:

(f) the interests of the person who provided the information where that person –

   (i)   was not under, or could not have been put under, any legal obligation to supply it to that or any other authority;

   (ii) did not supply it in any circumstances such that that or any other public authority is entitled apart from these Regulations to disclose it; and

   (iii) has not consented to its disclosure.

(EIR 2004, r. 12(5))

Therefore this covers cases where an individual has voluntarily reported a breach of an environmental issue on the understanding that the information will not be released. This would therefore protect any informants who reported breaches of environmental legislation.

10.3.15 Regulation 12(5)(g) Protection of the environment

This regulation allows information to be withheld for the protection of the environment, such as the location of badger setts or protected wild flowers. Care must be taken, however, to be consistent with this exemption and to apply it fairly to all requesters.

10.4   Summary

The purpose of information rights law is to make information accessible, and the many exemptions and exceptions exist to prevent inappropriate release of certain types of information. The intention of this chapter has been to enable authorities to identify where an exemption or exception may apply and to use it appropriately. Not all the exemptions will apply to all public authorities and many will need the application of the public interest test. How and when to apply the public interest test is the subject of the next chapter.

11

The public interest test

11.1 Introduction

Section 2(1) of the Freedom of Information Act 2000 and Regulation 12(1)(b) of the Environmental Information Regulations 2004 both direct that the public interest test must be applied to exemptions – to all in the case of Environmental Information Regulations.

Under the Freedom of Information Act there are certain exemptions to which the public interest does not apply. These are referred to under Section 2(3) as absolute exemptions. They are listed below in Table 11.1.

Table 11.1 Absolute exemptions under the Freedom of Information Act 2000

Section	Exemptions
Section 21	Information accessible by other means
Section 23	Information supplied by or relating to bodies dealing with security matters
Section 32	Court records
Section 34	Parliamentary privilege
Section 36	Prejudice to effective conduct of public affairs (House of Commons and House of Lords only)
Section 40	Personal data
Section 41	Provided in confidence
Section 44	Other legal prohibition on disclosure

All the remaining exemptions under the Freedom of Information Act are subject to the public interest test. They are listed in Table 11.2.

Table 11.2 Exemptions under the Freedom of Information Act 2000 where the public interest test must be applied

Section	Exemption
Section 22	Information intended for future publication
Section 24	National security (other than that covered by Section 23)
Section 26	Defence
Section 27	International relations
Section 28	Relations between the regional administrations in the United Kingdom
Section 29	The United Kingdom economy
Section 30	Investigations carried out by a public authority
Section 31	Law enforcement
Section 33	Audit functions by an external auditor
Section 35	Formulation of government policy
Section 36	Prejudice to the effective conduct of public affairs and inhibition of free and frank debate (but not Houses of Parliament)
Section 37	Communications with Her Majesty etc. and honours
Section 38	Health and safety
Section 39	Environmental information (because all exceptions are subject to the test)
Section 42	Legal professional privilege
Section 43	Commercial interest

11.2   When and who applies the test?

The first stage is to identify an exemption (or exception), for without one there is no test to apply. Start by asking, 'If there were no public interest test would this exemption be sufficient reason for withholding the data?' This can be answered by applying a 'prejudice test'. If the information were released would it prejudice either the authority or someone else? It is important to remember that there is no exemption for embarrassment.

If it is established that the exemption stands, then the request for information should be passed on to another person or group who can look at the public interest test. It is usually better for this person to have not been involved in the original application of the exemption because this allows for a completely independent view on the case. Also, the application of the test is looking at other issues than the application of exemptions, so having a separate person or group maintains this impartial approach.

Some public authorities have a board of senior managers to examine each case requiring the test. The case is presented by the person who has applied the exemption and the board decides on the public interest test. Care should be taken here that the board is mindful of the duty to release rather than withhold information. In some authorities the head of section applies the test after the exemption has been applied by others in the section.

The first approach has the advantage of involving more than one person in the decision, so the test can be discussed. It is the responsibility of senior management to appoint people to this function who know the legislation, whose job description includes the function, and who have an obligation to meet with others to deal with the questions when they come up. The single-person approach has the potential advantages that a consistent view should be obtained because only one person is involved who should have a good knowledge of the legislation. Such vital functions should never be the responsibility of a single person: there should always be a back-up or deputy.

11.3   What is the test?

Having established that the exemption is applicable the actual application of the test must be looked at. Because each request for information is different the public interest test may apply differently on each occasion. The test may be applied to a request and in six months' time the same test can be applied again with a different result. The test being applied is: 'Is it more in the public interest to withhold information than to release it?' The expectation is always that data will be released rather than withheld, even if an exemption can apply. If, when balancing the two sides of the question for or against release, the two sides are equal, then there is a duty to release.

The Information Commissioner has produced a list of issues that he considers should be taken into account when applying the test. The first is that the release of data should further the understanding of and participation in the public debate of issues of the day. Obviously this will change as local circumstances change, as the next example shows.

A new road was being designed although the actual route had not been decided. A proposal was submitted to the government and there was a strong probability of its changing the route.

A request for the submission was made by a lady whose house was next to the proposed route. The information was refused on the grounds that the proposal was still in draft (Environmental Information Regulations 12(4)(d)) and that to release it could blight property interests unnecessarily, as the route could still change. The Information Commissioner's Office disagreed and suggested that the report should be issued with the parts that could change being highlighted and the requester being told not to rely on the data. The Information Commissioner's view was that there was a great deal of public interest in the route and this outweighed the possibility of blight to property.

There is a requirement when replying to the requester to inform them not only that the test has been applied, but how it has been applied.

The second issue is to promote accountability and transparency on the part of public authorities for decisions taken by them. As public authorities are accountable for their actions, this is a good test to apply. The more open an authority, the fewer the problems with accusations of secrecy; and the more people understand why decisions are made, the less they are likely to question them.

The third issue is very similar, in promoting accountability and transparency in the spending of public funds.

The fourth issue is to allow individuals to understand decisions made by public authorities that affect their lives and, in some cases, to assist individuals in challenging those decisions. These matters are closely related and it can be seen from them that the information release can be very time dependent.

The last issue relates to bringing to light information affecting public safety, as this would outweigh any consideration of an exemption. The well-being of the public must come first.

11.4   Summary

The intention of the public interest test is to increase accountability, and probably means a complete culture change within public authorities. There is still reluctance to be open and to inform the public of decision-making processes. For this the reason it is recommended that application of the public interest test, and even of the exemptions, be done by a person or group completely independent of the team that generated the information.

There should be a commitment to implement a consistent and fair approach to the application of the public interest test. It should be remembered that requests are received purpose-blind and, as such, all potential uses of the data should be taken into account. Failure to do this could lead to a prejudicial application of the tests.

Under both the Freedom of Information Act 2000 and the Environmental Information Regulations 2004 there is either an exemption or an exception that allows for information which is already available elsewhere to be exempt under the legislation. There is a requirement to produce a schedule of such publicly available information, and this is explained in the next chapter.

12

Publication schemes

12.1 Introduction

The Freedom of Information Act places a duty on all public authorities to produce a publication scheme that shows what information is readily available to the public and it requires that any such scheme be approved by the Information Commissioner:

> 19(1) It shall be the duty of every public authority –
>
> (a) to adopt and maintain a scheme which relates to the publication of information by the authority and is approved by the Commissioner (in this Act referred to as a 'publication scheme'),
>
> (b) to publish information in accordance with the scheme and
>
> (c) from time to time review its publication scheme.
>
> (FOIA 2000, s. 19)

This is the first part of section 19, which relates to the duty to have a scheme. The title 'Publication Scheme' may suggest that only those documents and information that are printed and bound are properly published, but this is not the case. The scheme should cover all information that is readily available to the public, whether it is in a nicely bound booklet, a computer printout, or on the authority's website.

New information will be continually being created and it is for this reason that the Act directs that the scheme should be regularly updated to ensure that the latest information is available in the scheme.

Section 19 also points out that it is not sufficient just having the information listed in the scheme and that the information must be readily available. It is suggested to make occasional spot checks on the scheme to ensure that the information is available on demand from the locations stated.

It will also be noted that the scheme has to be approved by the Information Commissioner (see Chapter 13).

12.2   What the scheme should contain

For a legal explanation of what a scheme must contain, reference must first be made to the legislation:

> 19(2) A publication scheme must –
>   (a) specify classes of information which the public authority publishes or intends to publish,
>   (b) specify the manner in which information of each class is, or is intended to be, published and,
>   (c) specify whether the material is, or is intended to be, available to the public free of charge or on payment.
>
> (FOIA 2000, s. 19)

This, then, provides an outline for the scheme. It will include the classes of information available, where it can be obtained and whether a fee is applicable.

Classes of information are not lists of the actual information itself. Lists can be provided but do not form part of the actual scheme. Classes are groupings or categories of information that have a common feature – although not all of the information under a particular class might be included in the scheme. If it is decided, for example, that one of the class headings is 'Information rights law' it is unlikely that every document under that heading would be released. Sub-classes can be created, showing what information is actually available, but without specifying individual documents.

The example below from Ashfield District Council, one of the model publication schemes, shows how this can work.

Category	YOU AND YOUR COMMUNITY – ENVIRONMENT – RECLYCLING
Class Name	A–Z OF RECYCLING
Class Description	GENERAL GUIDE TO THE RECYCLING OF HOUSEHOLD MATERIALS
Contact	xxx
Format	
Associated Documents	>General Guide To The Recycling Of Household Materials

Category	YOU AND YOUR COMMUNITY – ENVIRONMENT – AIR QUALITY
Class Name	AIR QUALITY REVIEW AND ASSESSMENT STAGES 1, 2 AND 3
Class Description	REPORTS MEASURING LOCAL AIR POLLUTANTS, SUMMARISING LEVELS OF ETC
Contact	xxx
Format	WEBSITE – SUMMARIES ONLY; HARD COPY – CHARGE MAY APPLY
Associated Documents	>Air Quality Review And Assessment – August 2001 – Stage 1 and 2 >Air Quality Review And Assessment – August 2001 – Stage 3

Category	YOU AND YOUR COMMUNITY – ENVIRONMENT – ALLOTMENTS
Class Name	ALOTTMENT AND PLOT HOLDERS GUIDANCE
Class Description	DOCUMENT CONTAINING THE OPERATING GUIDANCE FOR PLOT HOLDERS
Contact	xxx
Format	HARD COPY
Associated Documents	>Allotment And Plot Holders Guidance

Category	YOU AND YOUR COMMUNITY – ENVIRONMENT – CAR PARKS
Class Name	ASHFIELD DISTRICT COUNCIL OFF STREET PARKING PLACES ORDER
Class Description	N/A
Contact	xxx
Format	HARD COPY; WEBSITE – AVAILABLE AUG 2003
Associated Documents	>Ashfield District Council Off Street Parking Places Order 2000

The scheme should also include an introduction to the authority's work and a description of the complaints procedure the authority has adopted for information rights, in particular, for freedom of information and environmental information.

The Information Commissioner has stated that he intends to issue a 'Sector Publication Scheme Pack' (ICO Policy on Publication Schemes) for each area of the public sector which, he states, will identify a base-level requirement for schemes in each sector and also recommend additional classes of information for inclusion, based on best practice.

12.3 Making the scheme available

There are various suggestions for implementing schemes; some public authorities have completely interactive online schemes that link directly to the documents. The Information Commissioner is of the view that while schemes should be available online, they should also be available elsewhere. An interactive scheme may not be practical for smaller public authorities such as parish councils, or for contractors such as doctors and dentists, although it can be very useful for larger authorities.

The Information Commissioner will be producing templates that will make the task easier for those authorities that were not given templates in the first round. He will also be issuing further guidance, based on experience gained in the first round of schemes.

12.4 Summary

A very basic publication scheme is all that is necessary, although this will be of little use to the public or even to the authority itself. A well-planned scheme can be viewed as a useful tool to help find data and avoid duplication, as part of the authority's asset register, and as a uscful customer service so that service users can find their own answers to questions – which will also save on staff time.

There are even suggestions that publication schemes should be combined with the information asset register required under the Re-use of Public Sector Information Regulations 2005, although this is still only at the ideas stage.

All publication schemes have to be approved by the Information Commissioner, so in the next chapter the roles of the Commissioner and the Information Tribunal will be examined.

13

Compliance, the Information Commissioner and the Information Tribunal

13.1 Introduction

In 1984 the role of Data Protection Registrar was created. This role continued under the Data Protection Act 1998, although the title was changed to that of Data Protection Commissioner (section 6). In 2000 with the introduction of the Freedom of Information Act, the title was changed again – to encompass the other two elements of information rights legislation – to that of Information Commissioner (Freedom of Information Act section 18). The title of the Data Protection Tribunal continued from 1984 until 2000, when it too had a name change, to that of Information Tribunal (FOIA 2000, s. 18).

Compliance does not involve just these two authorities, as there are issues that will be dealt with by the public authority itself and others that need reference to the courts.

The role of the Commissioner is not only to administer and police the legislation but also to advise and assist authorities in its application. His office is not a government department or agency but completely independent, although finance is still received from the Ministry of Justice.

13.2 Compliance

Enforcement of all sections of the legislation is carried out by the

Information Commissioner and failure to comply with his notices can be an offence.

Under the Freedom of Information Act there is only one criminal offence – that of changing, amending or removing data after a request has been made (section 77). The Environmental Information Regulations adds a further offence, that of obstructing the execution of a warrant.

There are considerably more offences under the Data Protection Act: processing data without it being on the register; failure to notify changes to the notification (section 21); and knowingly or recklessly obtaining or using data without consent of the data controller (section 55), to mention but two sections. Penalties are a fine, currently to a maximum of £5000, for each occasion there is a breach, plus the possibility of costs (section 60); or a period of imprisonment (as amended in 2007). It is also an offence to require that an individual provide 'relevant records' as a condition of employment or as a condition of contract (section 56). The Act describes relevant records as convictions or cautions issued by the police or the DHSS. The Act also voids any contract which requires a person to supply information they have obtained under section 7 of the Data Protection Act or any health record (section 57).

There are many examples of breaches which have resulted in fines. These range from local councillors obtaining personal data to help with election campaigns, individuals using data for their own gain, and individuals passing on information unthinkingly, anticipating that they were being of assistance, as in the following examples.

A young man dealt with a young female customer, made up his notes afterwards and then took the phone number and rang her asking for a date. She refused three times and eventually complained. The young man was dismissed and investigated under section 55 of the Data Protection Act.

A young woman was in dispute with her ex-partner. One Saturday the ex-partner's new girlfriend went round and shouted at the young woman on her doorstep, 'I work for the council and I know you owe over a hundred pounds council tax and that you are on benefits'. (Victim did not want to proceed but the girlfriend was dismissed from the council.)

And finally:

A teller at a building society spotted a young person they knew entering the building. The teller advised the person to think about moving home as the building society was to foreclose on the landlord. He was very upset, so was his landlord because he was not aware of this. (£5,000 fine plus costs.)

Action in such cases can only be taken by the Director of Public Prosecutions (DPP) or the Information Commissioner (section 60). There are also civil routes for individuals who have been wronged through an authority's not taking action under the Act, and there are sections that permit the courts to issue orders to ensure compliance (section 11, Direct marketing, for example). The penalty for non compliance (contempt) is two years' imprisonment, a fine, or both.

13.2.1 Complaints

Wherever possible, a complaint should be made to the authority; in fact this is a requirement under the Freedom of Information Act. Each authority must have a separate team where complaints are heard and only in exceptional circumstances should these be dealt with by the same person who made the original decision. The system must be impartial and must be seen to be so.

The officer dealing with the appeal may have little knowledge of the subject but can, of course, take advice, and it is sometimes better for a different viewpoint to be expressed. The Information Commissioner advises that the appeals officer should be senior to the officer making the initial decision. In cases of possible breaches of the Acts it is advisable to have an officer who is very familiar with the legislation (they will rarely be investigating their own area of work).

13.3   The Information Commissioner

13.3.1 Overview

The role of the Commissioner is best explained at schedule 5 of the Data

Protection Act 1998. It states clearly that he is not a servant of the Crown (Data Protection Act 1998, schedule 5(1)(2)) but an independent authority, even though the office is run with monies voted to it through the Ministry of Justice. He is, however, a public authority under the definition of the Freedom of Information Act. There have been occasions when he has had to criticize himself for breaching the legislation. Most Commissioners in other European countries are not covered by this type of Act.

The Information Commissioner is appointed to office for a period of five years and can be reappointed to two further periods of office, or until he is 65 whichever is the earlier, unless the public interest dictates otherwise.

The role of deputy commissioner is the only other position in the Information Commissioner's Office that has statutory basis. All other staff are appointed on a basis of need. Section 51 of the Data Protection Act and section 47 of the Freedom of Information Act start off in a very similar manner:

> (1) It shall be the duty of the Commissioner to promote the following of good practice by data controllers (public authorities) and, in particular, so to perform his functions under this Act as to promote the observance by data controllers (public authorities) of –
> (a) the requirements of this Act, and
> (b) the codes of practice under Sections 45 and 46.
>
> (DPA 1998, s. 51(1) and FOIA 2000, s. 47)

The next section directs that the Commissioner will disseminate information and good practice. From this it will be seen that the role of the Commissioner is not only to enforce the requirements of the Acts but also to promote the legislation and best practice

He may, with the consent of a public authority, assess that authority for good practice under the Freedom of Information Act and Environmental Information Regulations and he may, if he wishes, charge a fee for this. However, if the assessment of the public authority relates to the codes of practice under section 46 (Records management) he must consult with

The National Archives. Under section 48 of the Freedom of Information Act he can issue a code of practice without the consent of the authority. In this case the practice recommendation, as it is called, must relate to a particular area where, in the Commissioner's opinion, there is a need of best practice and he must consult The National Archives if it relates to records management. There has been an increasing number of cases where the Commissioner has issued practice notices either on the direction of the Information Tribunal or following his own investigations.

Under section 55 of the Freedom of Information Act the Commissioner also has powers of entry to premises to inspect information and, under schedule 9 of the Data Protection Act 1998, and schedule 3 of the Freedom of Information Act 2000, it is an offence to obstruct him in this duty.

Under the Data Protection Act the Commissioner is encouraged to liaise with trade authorities to encourage best practice. The National Archives also issues guidance on this area.

Both enactments state that the Commissioner must report annually to the House of Commons as to the exercise of his functions during the past year. His report is quite readable and often gives actual case studies, which are invaluable as training aids.

13.3.2 Complaints and decision notices

Under the Freedom of Information Act the Commissioner is required to review any complaint made against a public authority where the complainant believes that there has been a breach of the Act or the Environmental Information Regulations. The Commissioner has only four grounds for not looking into a complaint:

that the complainant has not exhausted any complaints procedure which is provided by the public authority in conformity with the codes of practice under section 45,

(a) that there has been undue delay in making the application

(b) that the application is frivolous or vexatious or

(c) that the application has been withdrawn or abandoned.

(FOIA 2000, s. 50)

This shows the importance of having a robust complaints procedure, although it is noticed that the Commissioner will attempt to resolve any complaints informally before proceeding to the more formal stages.

If necessary the Commissioner will issue a decision notice showing his decision and also any steps he requires the public authority to take, and stating the time limit for compliance. He may agree with parts of the complaint and not others. For example, he may agree that the authority was out of time but did apply an exemption correctly, or he may even dismiss a complaint as not upheld. At the informal stage he may agree that a breach has occurred but that the authority has done everything it can to rectify the problem and so no further action is necessary.

There is a right of appeal to the Information Tribunal both for the complainant and for the public authority (see below, 13.4).

13.3.3 Information notices

Under the Freedom of Information Act the Commissioner may issue an information notice (section 51) which compels a public authority to provide him with the information he requires to conduct his investigation into a complaint. It is interesting to note that the Commissioner may not require any communication that may be regarded as legal professional privilege. The definition of information also includes unrecorded information.

Failure to comply with an information notice may occur when a public authority:

(a) makes a statement which it knows to be false in a material respect, or
(b) recklessly make a statement which is false in a material way.

(FOIA 2000, s. 45(2))

13.3.4 Enforcement notices

If an authority fails to comply with a decision notice the Commissioner can issue an enforcement notice. Failure to comply with this is contempt of court (section 54(3)).

Government departments can obtain a ministerial certificate (see paragraph 10.2.5, Chapter 10), provided that such a certificate has been presented to Parliament, which would override either a decision notice or an enforcement notice. For the rest of the public sector a decision notice is a 'Just do it!' and an enforcement notice is a 'Definitely just do it!' The Commissioner can report a public authority to the courts for a breach of a decision notice, an enforcement notice or an information notice. He can also mention the authority in his report to Parliament.

13.3.5 Notices under the Data Protection Act

Under the Data Protection Act the Commissioner has powers to create enforcement notices and information notices (sections 40 and 43) that operate in a similar way to those of the Freedom of Information Act. In issuing an enforcement notice the Commissioner may take into account any damage and distress the complainant has been caused, when he decides on the seriousness of the case. The information notice cannot ask for information that is covered by legal privilege or for information that would reveal evidence of the authority committing an offence, excepting one caused under the Data Protection Act.

Section 47(3) provides a defence against failure to disclose, in that the person exercised due diligence to comply with the notice. In other words, it would have to be proved that the failure to disclose was carried out on purpose.

13.3.6 The Office of the Commissioner

The main office of the Information Commissioner is at Wycliffe House, Water Lane, Wilmslow, Cheshire SK9 5AF. He also has offices in Scotland: 28 Thistle Street Edinburgh EH2 1EN; Cardiff: Cambrian Buildings, Mount Stuart Square, Cardiff CF10 5FL; Belfast: Room 101 Regus House, 33 Clarendon Dock, Laganside, Belfast BT1 3BG, and a small office in London.

The Office has a help desk function. The data protection and the freedom of information functions are separate from each other and the Freedom of Information Act function is divided into advice and enforcement. This may change in future, and authority areas such as for the finance sector, local government and central government and so on could be established.

13.4   The Information Tribunal

In cases of disagreement with the decisions of the Information Commissioner there is a form of appeal to the Information Tribunal. The appeal can be from either the complainant or the public authority and can be in relation to any of the information rights trilogy of legislation (see section 57 of the Freedom of Information Act or section 48 of the Data Protection Act). It is interesting to note that very few cases are referred to the Tribunal in relation to data protection.

The complaints have to be, in the first instance, against the decision of the Information Commissioner and they are described as '*Complainant*' v. *Information Commissioner*. The Tribunal can add the public authority to the matter by a Notice of Joinder, which usually means the public authority is a co-defendant.

The Tribunal often holds pre meetings, with just the chair and the various parties, in an attempt to resolve any issues without going to a full tribunal. These hearings are nonetheless relatively formal and the Commissioner is usually represented by a solicitor and a barrister. While there is no requirement for the public authority to have legal representation at this stage it is advisable. The complainant can represent themself as 'litigant in person'.

A full Tribunal hearing consists of the chair and two other representatives, one from the area the public authority is in, and one from the complainant's side. The Tribunal is conducted as a court, and witness evidence can be called and given under oath. The chair can ask for the hearing to be conducted by video or audio link if he prefers, but if any party objects a full hearing has to take place.

The Tribunal's findings are binding, although they can be contested on a point of law in the courts. The Tribunal is completely independent of the Commissioner's Office and has its office in Leicester. Not all the findings of the Tribunal uphold the decisions of the Commissioner.

The costs of attending the Tribunal can be quite high for a public authority, as barristers do not come cheaply, and a case can result in adverse publicity.

Section 6 and Schedule 5 part II of the Data Protection Act 1998 describe the creation of the Tribunal. The description is continued and slightly amended by section 2 of the Freedom of Information Act.

There have been some interesting decisions from the Tribunal which have helped in the definition of data and the procedures of the Freedom of Information Act and the Environmental Information Regulations. Two in particular have had a major impact. The first decision was against Royal Mail and relates to access to backup files if they are easily accessible. The second is the Markinson case, in which the level of fees for supplying information under the Environmental Information Regulations was set (see Chapter 9.4).

13.5   Summary

The function of the Information Commissioner now has legislative teeth, unlike that of the old Data Protection Registrar, although the Commissioner prefers to sort out issues informally. There are an increasing number of decisions and it is recommended that you take full advantage of the service provided by the Commissioner's website (www.ico.gov.uk) to search for the latest decisions in your particular area of interest.

Another way of finding out how authorities are doing is to look at their disclosure logs, which are explained in the next chapter.

14

Disclosure logs

14.1 Introduction

There is no legal requirement for any public authority to have a disclosure log although a Best Practice Guidance on the subject was issued by the Department for Constitutional Affairs in December 2005.

An individual can make a request under the Freedom of Information Act 2000 or the Environmental Information Act 2004 for information held by a public authority and they must be told, in most cases, whether or not the information is held and, if information is withheld, the reasons why it is withheld.

The authority probably already has a record of the requests it has received and how they were handled, including the date of receipt and the response given. This might be anything from a paper record to a fully comprehensive workflow management system on the computer. A disclosure log is the base data extracted from this record and made available to the public.

14.2 Benefits

Why should this information be made available? The purpose of the Freedom of Information Act and the Environmental Information Regulations is to make as much information available as possible, and frequently the same or similar requests will be made by a number of separate individuals – local authority staff will have lost count of the number of requests relating to topics such as cooling towers, for example. Similarly the courts have recognized that once information has been released under the Freedom of Information Act it is in the public domain, copyright etc. notwithstanding. As requests are received purpose-blind any information that is released can be used for whatever purpose the requester wishes, provided that the copyright laws are not breached.

A disclosure log can make information available to a wider audience as repeat requests can be directed to the log. Information made available in this way is eligible for a section 21 exemption (see paragraph 10.2.1, Chapter 10). This will save time for the authority in providing the information again (unless it has changed substantially) and enable a faster response to the requester.

Providing information freely in this way also helps dispel the perception of secrecy that often surrounds the public sector. Those who wish to know how an authority is handling certain matters can have easy access to items in the the decision-making process which another person has already requested. It also assists continuity across the authority for other members of staff to see how exemptions are being applied and ensures that a similar approach is being followed across the whole authority.

Disclosure logs can be a user-friendly way for the public to access information and are beneficial for an authority as it strives to meet the target of being more open and accountable.

14.3   Scope

There is no requirement to have a disclosure log and the content of the log is very much up to the individual authority.

Various approaches can be adopted, from a very basic list of requests that the authority regards as being of most interest to the public, to an online interactive system that not only lists all the requests made, why information was redacted and the response, but also links to a copy of the actual information released.

A great deal will depend on the size of the authority. A parish council has far fewer resources and will have far fewer requests than a government department. It might not be practical, if a great many requests were received, to release all the information through the log, as there would be too much information for the next requester to search through. If, on the other hand, only a few requests are received, subject to the exemptions and other caveats (looked at in Chapter 14), it may be very straightforward to release all the information that was released to the first requester.

At the very least, the most high-profile cases should be made available, or those in which it is considered the public will have the most interest. Only the authority can judge what is top of the agenda in its area at any given time. The numbers of requests being received for information on different subjects will give an idea of what to make available.

The log need not be solely for releasing information that has been requested, it can also be a tool for proactively disseminating information to the public where it is anticipated that interest will follow. This could be about the building of a new road, or a school merger. If the information is released on how decisions are made before requests are received, many future requests can be saved. It is appreciated that this will mean a complete change of culture for many public authorities, but the purpose of the legislation is to make information more readily available.

If the information has already been made available elsewhere, the log can provide an interactive link to it, or at least an indication of where the information can be found. As will be realized, there is a great deal of similarity and interaction between the log and the authority's publication scheme (see Chapter 12).

However, the log should not be seen as a way of not responding to an initial request. If information has been requested that is not on the log, in no way should it be added until it has been sent to the requester.

14.4   Restrictions

A few types of data are not appropriate for release to a wider audience. This could include third party data that is not exempt but that it would be inappropriate to release elsewhere, or information that has been obtained from another authority.

If an individual has been charged under the Freedom of Information

Act or the Environmental Information Regulations for the data (for either time or disbursements), it would be most improper to release the information free of charge to everyone else. It may be possible, however, to state what charge will be made if anyone else wishes to see the data. This could then be included in the publication scheme.

Any personal data must be handled in accordance with the Data Protection Act 1998 and should, in most cases, have already been exempted under section 40 of the Freedom of Information Act or regulation 13 of the Environmental Information Regulations, but the data protection principles must be taken into account. An individual may have reasonably expected that details were given to an individual requester but not made generally available.

Breaches of copyright are discussed in Chapter 15, but at this point it should be remembered that releasing information under the Freedom of Information Act to an individual is not a breach of copyright law, but this may not be the case for information released to a wider audience.

14.5   What goes into a disclosure log?

The disclosure log should be easy to read and simple to use, otherwise it will not be used. The phrases and abbreviations used should be meaningful, and not just public authority jargon.

The log should be a gateway to the information, preferably by computer link, so the information at the end of the link must also be readable. For example, if a document is in PDF format there should be a way of downloading a free PDF reader such as Adobe Acrobat. There may be problems if the documents are stored in Microsoft Word format because not everyone will have access to Microsoft products. File sizes should also be as small as is practical to allow the viewer access over a slow internet connection. If documents are not held electronically a practical solution could be to scan in the data or allow the requester to request it by e-mail.

The log should also be easily accessible via a link from at least the Freedom of Information page of the authority's website, but preferably also from the home page of the website. The Ministry of Justice recommends using the title 'Freedom of Information disclosure', to achieve some level of consistency across the public sector.

A list of disclosures on its own does not provide the requester with a great deal of information. The method of listing will depend on how many requests it is intended to log. If there are not many, then a list in chronological order may be sufficient; for a large number of requests it may be more useful to sort them by subject or interest. The same categories used for the publication scheme could be used, for the sake of consistency. If the log is computerized, a search engine will also be very useful.

Instead of providing access to the information that has been released, a very short summary may answer many questions. There is a good example of this method on the website for the Ministry of Defence disclosure log, www.mod.gov.uk/publications/Freedom of Information Act/rr/rrsep05. htm.

14.6   Maintenance

It is no good having a very good log which was only up to date on the day it was launched. Resources should be allocated to ensure that the log is kept up to date and information added or removed regularly. The Ministry of Justice recommends that the list be reviewed at least monthly, and that the same person be responsible for checking the authority's publication scheme at the same time to ensure the two work together. It even goes so far as to suggest a job description for this position:

- Raising awareness of the disclosure log across the whole of the public authority, ensuring staff consider whether information they hold and create could be pro-actively published on the disclosure log;
- Monitoring information requests being processed within the public authority and identifying whether information could be pro-actively published on the disclosure log;
- Managing and organising the content of the disclosure log, identifying new categories of information to ensure that disclosure logs are organised in a user friendly format;
- Updating the disclosure log regularly with new releases;

- Removing and archiving, where appropriate, older information disclosures to save server space. Information archived in this way should still be accessible on request.

(DCA Code of Practice on Disclosure Logs, December 2005)

Information can be removed if the interest has ceased or the information has been superseded and is therefore misleading.

14.7   Summary

Disclosure logs have benefits for the requester and also for the public authority, and they can be operated in conjunction with the publication scheme, but they do have to be kept up to date. The Ministry of Justice suggests some sites which are currently good examples of best practice, including that of the Ministry of Defence.

Many of the principles of a disclosure log are covered by good records management procedures, and these are covered in the next chapter.

15

Records management – Section 46 code of practice

15.1 Introduction

Records management is a complete and complex topic in its own right and there are many books and papers already written on the subject. It is not the intention here to replace these publications but to explain, using the code of practice issued under section 46 of the Freedom of Information Act 2000 and guidance issued by The National Archives as a basis, how a public authority must apply the basic principles of records management in the context of information rights.

Good records management is the keystone to the effective management of information rights legislation. Without well-managed records the information that is requested cannot be accessed. A speaker from The National Archives, Susan Healy, states that 'Records management can survive without information rights but information rights cannot survive without records management'.

There are specific requirements for records management under the information rights legislation. The Data Protection Act 1998 requires under data protection principle 3 that data are adequate and not excessive, under principle 4 that they are accurate and up to date, under principle 5 that they are not kept longer than is necessary and under principle 7 that they are safeguarded from unauthorized access and use. All of these are elements of good records management which are reflected in the code of practice on records management that the Freedom of Information Act

2000 (section 46) required the Lord Chancellor to issue. The Environmental Information Regulations 2004 also contain requirements affecting
records management: regulation 4, for example, requires information to
be organized so that it can be easily disseminated and available
electronically.

Any organization, whether it is a major public authority or a doctor's
surgery, needs to be able to access accurate and reliable records and the
code sets out the good practice to achieve that end as well as to support
compliance with information rights legislation. Although the code of
practice is intended for public authorities covered by the Freedom of
Information Act and other bodies that are subject to the Public Records
Acts, it is a useful guide and framework to build the management of
records in all organizations. It must not be seen as just another code which
has to be complied with, but as an invaluable aid to successfully managing
records.

15.2   Purposes and scope of the code

Part I of the code gives a basic framework of good practice for records
management in public authorities. Part II deals with the practices that
public record bodies (bodies subject to the Public Records Acts) should
follow for transferring records to The National Archives, the Public
Record Office of Northern Ireland or another archives office appointed
to hold public records.

The code points out that further guidance can be obtained from
published standards (a list of the more pertinent is given in Appendix 3 of
this book). A series of implementation guides written by Margaret Crockett
is published by The National Archives and is extremely useful if embarking
on this area. They cover 'What is Records Management?', 'Records
Management Policy', 'Human Resources in Records Management',
'Active Records Management: Records Creation', 'Active Records
Management: Record Keeping and Record Maintenance' and 'Disposal
Arrangements' and are available for free from The National Archives'
website (see Appendix 5).

The code of practice suggests that other named pieces of legislation relating to information be read in conjunction with the code of practice. Another set of regulations passed since the code was issued should also be considered, the Re-use of Public Sector Information Regulations 2004 (See Chapter 16.4)

The code states that its aims are:

(1) to set out practices which public authorities and bodies subject to the Public Records Act 1958 and the Public Records Act (Northern Ireland) 1923, should follow in relation to the creation, keeping, management and destruction of their records (Part One of the Code), and
(2) to describe the arrangements which public records bodies should follow in reviewing public records and transferring them to the Public Records Office or to places of deposit or to the Public Record Office of Northern Ireland (Part Two of the Code).

(Lord Chancellor's Code of Practice issued under
section 46 of the Freedom of Information Act 2000)

The code covers all records, no matter how they are kept. In fact, it refers to records in all technical or physical formats, which includes paper, microfilm, electronic records, etc. It applies to records at all stages of their life, from inception to transfer to an archives office or destruction; but it does not extend to records after they have been permanently archived; the code stops at the point of transfer.

Although there is a duty in the Freedom of Information Act to issue a code of practice, compliance with it is not mandatory. However, if the code were to be breached there would be a strong probability of a breach of some other records management legislation.

While the Information Commissioner is responsible for promoting and monitoring good practice under the code, investigations into infringements of the code must involve The National Archives where public record bodies are involved. Where the Information Commissioner issues a practice recommendation (section 48) for records management issues he must consult the Keeper of Public Records if public records are involved, or the Keeper of Public Records (Northern Ireland) if the records are kept by a body subject to that act. There is also an agreement between The

National Archives and the Information Commissioner's Office that The National Archives will provide advice and assistance in relation to records management in other organizations.

The code highlights the connection between records management and information rights, emphasizing the importance to information rights of the good keeping of records, by stating:

> It is desirable that the person or persons responsible for the Records Management function should also have either direct responsibility or an organisational connection with the person or persons responsible for freedom of information, data protection and other information management issues.
>
> (Lord Chancellor's Code of Practice issued under section 46 of the Freedom of Information Act 2000)

15.3   Basic requirements of records management

15.3.1   Overview

The guides define records management as

> The function of creating, organising and maintaining records to ensure they provide evidence of activity, decision making and policy. It includes the establishment of links between related records, swift and accurate filing and accessibility when required and scheduled destruction or transfer to an archives repository as appropriate in a timely fashion. The term 'record keeping' is often used interchangeably with Records Management.
>
> (Lord Chancellor's Code of Practice issued under section 46 of the Freedom of Information Act 2000)

From this it can be seen that records management is not just about filing and being able to retrieve records but also about how they are created, destroyed and interact with other records, all absolutely vital when retrieving information following a request.

The code of practice makes the point that records management should be a corporate system, not individual or personal filing systems:

The Estates section of a local authority had a corporate filing system in which all transactions were to be kept and this was maintained by a team of filing clerks. Unfortunately individual officers did not trust the system as it was felt that it was incomplete and, while still complying with the corporate system, they also kept in their desk drawers personal copies of all correspondence, and notes which gave their personal records a fuller story of the particular situation.

Records start life as live files, when they are being handled almost daily. Following this they become dormant, when they have ceased to be added to, but may still be required for reference so are retained. At the end of this stage they should be considered for destruction, extended retention for reference purposes, or transfer to an archives service, either in-house or external. Which action to apply will depend on the nature and continued usefulness of the records.

15.3.2 Policy

A records management policy should clearly define the responsibilities and objectives (and resources) needed to achieve effective management. The second implementation guide published by The National Archives defines a records management policy as

> a document, which serves as a mandate for managing records in the organization. It is a statement that describes what the organization does and intends to do with respect to its records. It underpins a Records Management programme, giving it authority and emphasising its importance in an organization.
>
> (TNA Records Management Guides:
> Records Management Policy (Crocker, 2006))

Therefore, not only is a policy a requirement of the code of practice, it is also a vital document for any organization. As such, it should be approved and receive full commitment at the highest possible level in any organization, and staff should be made aware of its requirements. It should cover, at a high level, all aspects of the records' life, as these are the lifeblood of any organization, regardless of its size. Like information rights, the records management policy should not stand alone but form an integral part of an organization's core policies, with cross references to related policies on, for example, information security, access and data protection, which rely on records to function.

Any organization should show its commitment to good records and information management and set out how it intends to create, keep and manage its records. The policy will, according to the code, define the organization's strategy, roles and responsibilities for record keeping and give guidance and direction on issues such as retention periods. It will also state how the standards that have been prepared are to be adopted and monitored.

Any such policy needs regular review, which the code of practice currently suggests should be every three years. Future versions of the code may amend this by extending the time or suggesting that the organization's circumstances be taken into account. Any new policy needs to take into account ISO 15489 and other standards issued or amended since the code of practice was published. It is recommended that those in an organization who are responsible for records management are fully trained in all aspects of any new standards so that the organization is fully conversant with any new requirements.

Before embarking on developing a policy it is also recommended that a careful study is made of the guidance from The National Archives (found on the National Archives website under 'Services for Professionals – Records Management Code'), as this sets out the steps needed to create such a policy. Needless to say, the first item is the same as that for information rights: there is a requirement for senior management and political, if appropriate, 'buy in' to any policy for it to be successful.

15.3.3 Human resource issues

The code states that a senior designated member of staff should have the lead in records management. This officer will act as the Records Management Champion. The actual management of the records should be carried out by a person who has the necessary skills and knowledge to manage the records. These skills should be incorporated into a job description. Obviously the size of the organization will have some bearing on salary and scope, and also on whether it will need a full-time records manager. Many organizations combine responsibility for records management with other information-related work, for example freedom of information and data protection, or archives. In smaller organizations the champion and the records management practitioner may be one and the same person.

Section 7.3 of the code of practice describes the requirements for a records manager. The paragraph emphasizes the need to have well-qualified staff who should be regarded as professionals in their own right. They should have similar professional development programmes to those that would be given to other professionals, such as architects and lawyers, and should be given the facilities to keep abreast of any new developments in the profession, such as electronic document management. A competency framework for records managers, such as the one provided by The National Archives, is recommended.

In large organizations there are likely to be three levels of staff involved in the management of records, as suggested in the third implementation guide from The National Archives. In smaller organizations such as parish councils, schools, or even the doctor's surgery it is more likely that one person will perform all these functions in addition to their other duties. Firstly there is the management level, where the policy, strategy and implementation in the organization will be promoted. This person is likely to be at board level as their function will be to present the policies to the board, the chief executive or elected representatives and to raise awareness of records management at the highest levels in the organization. Secondly there follows the practitioner level, the operational records manager who will actually implement the policy and ensure that supporting documents are in place, such as procedures, disposal schedules, etc. It is important to note that it is no good just appointing someone to do this work; they must be given the resources to be able to carry out their duties. The really successful organizations, such as certain county councils, have a well-qualified and enthusiastic records manager and staff to support the work of records management. Thirdly, all staff have to be aware of their responsibilities as they all create records and keep them as part of their daily work, especially where they are involved in some decision-making process such as planning or licensing, where an accurate and full record is needed of decisions made in case they are questioned at a later stage. Staff need to be given time to do this work and, the guide suggests, this should be written into their job descriptions to emphasize the importance of accurate and complete record keeping. Of course, this goes back to the underlying principle already examined under information rights, that of adequate training. The training should cover awareness and basic principles of effective records management, not necessarily going into the details as these will vary from post to post. Including records management training in induction training sessions for new staff, in combination with information rights awareness, should be considered, so that the links between the two can be pointed out. Neither temporary staff nor those who have been doing a job for years should be forgotten. Refresher sessions are always useful, especially if new technologies are being introduced, such as electronic documents and records management systems (EDRMS).

15.3.4 Active records management

It is important that every area of the organization has adequate systems in place to record its activities and decision-making processes. This is important not only because someone may ask for the information but also because without it the unit cannot operate properly. Each unit will have specific requirements depending on its own functions and its need to refer back to or explain its actions and decisions, but they should all be compliant with the organization's overall policy.

Purpose

The primary purpose of record keeping is to enable current and future employees to carry out their functions properly. Records providing information about past activities should be readily available to staff so that previous decision-making processes can be followed, thereby allowing for consistent decisions, and evidence of past decisions can be available should it be necessary to account for them in the future. It is this 'corporate memory' which is vital to the operation of any organization. To achieve it, the records must be accurate and complete, they should allow for a complete audit trail of actions taken to be undertaken, but also protect the legal and moral rights of the organization and of those whose data is being handled.

It almost goes without saying that the records must be easy to access. If time is wasted in accessing the records, then valuable resources can be lost or, if it seems more trouble than it is worth, incorrect decisions can be made.

Information audit

It is not possible to implement a reasonable records management system without knowing the scope of the records the organization needs and holds. Not only does it need to know what records it has but it also needs to know what, if any, records management arrangements are in place already that it can use as a foundation for further work. An information audit or survey will serve a number of purposes. Not only will it provide details of what records are kept, how they are used and for how long they need to be kept, it can also enable instances of duplication to be identified and eliminated and promote availability of more accurate information. This was proved by one authority on the introduction of a geographic information system (GIS).

A public authority held base maps for its patch. It had six different departments and this resulted in there being in excess of fourteen different versions of a base map for the district. Some showed the latest open spaces, others the latest roads and others the latest developments, but no map showed all these together in relation to each other. The authority purchased a corporate GIS and produced various layers for each of the departments so it was then possible to have one definitive map with the relationship between all these details shown, also saving thousands of pounds in duplicated work.

This illustration can also be applied to records management more widely, and an effective system can save the organization many thousand of pounds in staff time and resources. Not only will such an audit tell what an authority has, it can provide invaluable information on the quality of the records and even on how an organization works, showing how processes operate and how related information flows, for example. From this data it will be possible to improve the effectiveness and efficiency of services as well as to assist in the supply of data to provide answers to information rights questions.

Having established what there is (see Records Management Guide Number 5), it is necessary to look at consistency and standards, particularly in relation to referencing and titling. The code of practice itself does not give any guidance in this area other than to state that

These should be easily understood and should enable the effective retrieval of information.   (Lord Chancellor's Code of Practice issued under section 46 of the Freedom of Information Act 2000)

In the next part of this chapter (15.3.5) some guidance is given about the creation and referencing of records.

Storage

The code of practice gives some advice on the storage of records. It states that records should be stored safe from unauthorized access, in areas that meet current fire regulations and provide adequate protection from vermin and damp, both of which damage paper records in particular. Depending on their frequency of use, they also need to be easily accessible. It is suggested that, when access is infrequent, it may be more economical to store the records off-site, as this type of storage is often cheaper. If this is the case, it should be remembered that secure and adequate storage conditions will also need to be in place (see further under paragraph 15.3.5).

Emergencies

A contingency plan for action in the event of emergencies is needed. For example if a records storage area is affected by a flood, access and security arrangements will be needed, such as storing off-site or providing sealed rooms – the situation one council in the North West found itself in after a major flood, where records were kept in a basement and were destroyed when the town hall, the police station and the fire station were flooded. The code advises that

A contingency or business recovery plan should be in place for records which are vital to the continued functioning of the authority.

(Lord Chancellor's Code of Practice issued under section 46 of the Freedom of Information Act 2000)

Special attention should be given to vital records, which could be decisions, details of recent financial transactions, personnel records or asset records, for example. Only around 3% of records are likely to be vital, and they may not have long-term value; they may be vital for a limited time only and after that lose their importance to the organization. The test is: can the organization function without them? If yes, they are probably not vital. A separate test relates to the long-term value of the records to the organization; these records need to be saved also. Records falling into both categories should be clearly identified.

15.3.5 Creation and storage of records

Whenever a document is written and stored it is likely that a record has been created. Documents are created because there is a need or desire to record some action, to communicate something, or to provide an aide memoir. In other words there may be a need to refer back to it at some stage, to use the information or to explain previous actions. This is where records management comes in, because there needs to be some system in which to store and retrieve the document.

The secret to easy and speedy document retrieval is clear, uncomplicated referencing which everyone can easily understand and follow. Whenever a document is created there is also a need for some sort of referencing so that the record can be identified and recovered. A thing or subject can be described by many different words depending on usage, for example a person under 16 can be a child, a teenager, a youth, a young person, a student, a pupil or even an infant or baby. Searching for cross departmental records becomes very difficult if the same definitions are not used across the organization or there is not some corporate thesaurus to help identify these cross references. The word used must, however, be meaningful:

One chief constable did say, 'We must stop filing everybody under 'v' for villain'.

Not only should the record itself be easily identifable and understood, but so should its location and its status, whether it is the latest version, and who has seen it. This can be resolved by good records and document management functionality and the effective use of metadata to keep a track of versions and access. For both paper and electronic records, an auditable trail of the progress of the records is essential. It is necessary to know whether the document being recalled is the latest version, and for this the date and time of creation, in addition to the author and title, is required. It is often useful to know why it was created, e.g. a report to management team, a proposal, reminder etc., and this can be made part of the document title as well as specified in related metadata. It may be necessary to apply some sort of security or classification on the document, such as 'confidential', as required by the organization's policies. Again, this emphasizes the link between records management and other corporate policies in the organization.

The 'heap' principle of storage is unacceptable; records should be stored in an orderly fashion in a clean, uncluttered area with adequate protection from damage by fire, water and vermin. They should be readily accessible but should also be secure from unauthorized access, a requirement for personal data under the Data Protection Act (principle 7), and inactive records should be kept away from the normal work place to avoid clutter and confusion.

Horror stories abound about organizations who retain files in inaccessible places. It should be remembered that there is no point in keeping the record if it cannot be accessed.

A public authority had a spare chimney at the crematorium and used this to store its records. An education department kept its archive records in two walk-in skips in the car park.

15.3.6 Disposal and retention periods

Following the live and active part of a record's life it will need to be closed. According to Implementation Guide Number 6 there are four common triggers for closing records:

a) No action on the record – either addition of material or retrieval/access
b) End of project or cycle
c) The record exceeds a certain size (this size will depend on the format and purpose of the record)
d) Expiry of a number of years.

(TNA Disposal Arrangements, Guide No. 6 (Crocker, 2006))

Closed records will be disposed of after a retention period that is either specified in a disposal schedule or determined after evaluation of the records. Disposal here means either destruction or transfer to an archives service for permanent preservation.

The Freedom of Information Act makes the orderly disposal of records particularly important. It is an offence (section 77) to remove or destroy data to avoid answering a request, so it is vital that any destruction of records is properly recorded and follows corporate policy, so as to protect staff from being charged with an offence.

It is important that an organization has in place a policy outlining the types of records that will be selected for permanent preservation, and a retention or disposal schedule specifying the retention period for particular types of records and how they will be disposed of at the end of that period, i.e. whether they will be destroyed or transferred to an archives service for permanent preservation.

The schedule should take into account statutory arrangements and also operational requirements although the recommendation of 'indefinite' retention from a manager should not be accepted unless the term really means permanent preservation. If it is known that a document will, exceptionally, be needed after the scheduled destruction date, for example because there is a Freedom of Information appeal in progress or pending litigation, that date can be delayed and a new one assigned. This policy and the schedule should be endorsed at the very highest organizational level and staff should be made aware of their existence and encouraged to inform the records managers when they need to be updated because of changed circumstances.

There are various sources for retention schedules which can be used as a basis. Generic schedules are available from The National Archives (www.nationalarchives.gov.uk/recordsmanagement/advice/pdf/sched_disposal.pdf) and sector-specific schedules are available from the Records Management Society for local government records (www.rms–gb.org.uk/resources/91) and from sector-specific sources for other sectors, such as schedules for police forces from ACPO (www.acpo.police.uk/asp/policies/Data/MoPI%20Guidance_INTER_03.03.06.pdf), for higher education from JISC (www.jisc.ac.uk/index.cfm?name=srl_structure) and for the NHS from the Department of Health (www.dh.gov.uk/PublicationsAndStatistics/Publications/PublicationsPolicyAndGuidance/PublicationsAndPolicyGuidanceArticle/fs/en?CONTENT_ID=413`747&chk=tMmN39).

A schedule by itself may not be considered an adequate record of what records have been destroyed. Some evidence of implementation, such as a separate log, could be kept to show what has been destroyed, and under what authority. If records are being sent for destruction away from the organization's premises strict controls are needed, especially if personal data is involved, to ensure compliance with the data protection principle 7. Note that under the Data Protection Act an organization is responsible for breaches of this principle by a contractor destroying records on its behalf.

A journalist found a number of claims and returns relating to individuals' financial status on a main road leaving a major city in the Midlands. A government department had employed a contractor to remove and destroy old records from its headquarters in that city and the contractor had not kept them secure, so they were scattered along this road.

15.3.7 Electronic records

The principles behind the keeping of electronic records are similar to those for manual records. However, electronic records have particular character-istics and requirements that need to be reflected in their storage and management. The term 'electronic records' here means not only the docu-ments and other records kept on computers and servers but also e-mails, which have largely replaced memoranda and letters for written communications.

There is a temptation to keep electronic documents for longer than necessary because it is assumed that storage is much simpler and cheaper than for paper records. However, this is not necessarily the case because the processes associated with storage of electronic records over time carry costs. In any case, it is not good practice to keep information for longer than it is needed, for whatever purpose, so electronic records should be evaluated along the same lines as paper records. This applies also to e-mail, and those that are useful and meaningful should be kept, while those that are ephemeral or meaningless should be discarded. This process will be helped if good e-mail practice is in place covering, for example, responsibility for filing internal exchanges, the level of formality to be used, etc. The National Archives has published guidance on developing an e-mail policy which covers this type of good practice, see www.nationalarchives.gov.uk/documents/managing_emails.pdf.

Great care must be taken in how the records are kept if they are likely to be used again. How many people can still access Word Star and have access to a 5¼ inch disk drive? Even 3½ inch disks are becoming a thing of the past and what of the data stored on a version of Microsoft Word that is no longer supported? Moving data to new systems – migration – is an essential component of managing electronic records and needs to be carried out in an organized and auditable way if the migrated records are to be accepted as reliable and authentic.

Records should be kept in a clearly structured manner with meaningful titles. Documents filed under the user's name are, to all intents and purposes, hidden from everyone except that user but they may be crucial to the operation of the organization, so they should be filed somewhere accessible to colleagues and given meaningful titles so that work does not come to a halt during staff absences.

Before looking at the way in which electronic records are stored or acquiring an electronic document and records management system it is worth referring to The National Archives' website for details of its *Functional Requirements for Electronic Records Management Systems* (www.nationalarchives.gov.uk/electronicrecords/function.htm). It is very important to bear in mind that acquisition of an expensive electronic documents and records management system will not in itself solve all records management problems. Electronic systems can bring great benefits, but if the underlying procedures and good practices are not in place they will not provide the solutions sought.

The National Archives has issued a range of guidance on electronic Records Management – see www.nationalarchives.gov.uk/electronic records/?source=ddmenu_services2 – and relevant standards have been published by the British Standards Institute, in particular *Principles of Good Practice for Information Management – PD 0010* and *A code of Practice for Legal Admissibility and Evidential Weight of Information Stored Electronically* .

15.4   Review and transfer of public records

This part of the code of practice only relates to those public authorities subject to the Public Records Acts. These, in the main, are central government departments and dependent bodies, the courts, NHS and armed services.

Under public records legislation, public records selected for permanent preservation have to be transferred to either The National Archives or another approved place of deposit for public records or, if they are Northern Ireland public records, to the Public Record Office of Northern Ireland. Transfer must take place by the time the records are 30 years old, as a general rule (20 years for Northern Ireland records). The code of practice provides for records to be assessed before transfer in order to decide whether they should be transferred as 'open on transfer' or, if that is not possible, to identify which exemptions from disclosure apply and specify for how long they should continue to apply after transfer. Details are to be set out on a schedule and, if historical records are involved, the schedule is reviewed by the Advisory Council on National Records and Archives. Historical records are records that are over 30 years old and some of the exemptions cannot be used for historical records.

15.5   Summary

Effective records management is vital to the proper operation of all three of the main elements of information rights legislation. Without it, organizations will not be able to answer requests, nor will they be able to function effectively. The National Archives and the Records Management Society are always at hand to offer advice, and there are significant cost benefits for an organization if systems are implemented properly.

It must be remembered that an organization could be measured against the code of practice under section 46 and, if failings are identified, it could be subject to a formal Practice Recommendation issued by the Information Commissioner. The National Archives has produced a very effective audit document that will assist in identifying the gaps in current systems, and an excellent series of guides (as listed in paragraph 15.2) to help the non records manager to get started on this subject. These are available free of charge on their website (see Appendix 5).

There are other items of legislation that also have an effect on access to data and some of these will be looked at in the next chapter.

16

Other legislation

16.1 Introduction

All information rights legislation, with the exception of the Environmental Information Regulations, takes second place to other statutes. Thus, if another statute states that data must or must not be shared, the Freedom of Information Act and the Data Protection Act may not apply. Similarly, under the Data Protection Act, the exemptions for non disclosure apply only to that Act, and there must be other legislation that permits the data to be shared in the first place. It would be difficult to provide a definitive list of the legislation that may apply, but some was mentioned in Chapter 7; it includes the Crime and Disorder Act 1998, Children and Adoptions Act and other Children's Acts, and the Local Government Acts (particularly 2000).

Under the Freedom of Information Act care must be taken to conform with the Enterprise Act 2002 before sharing data; and under the Data Protection Act you may need to take the Finance Act 1988, the Local Government Finance Act 1992, the Local Government Act 2002 and the Housing Act 2004 into consideration. These were explained in Chapters 6 and 10. When releasing documents account must be taken of the various copyright Acts, in particular the Copyright, Designs and Patents Act 1988 (as amended).

There are some other Acts and regulations on the periphery of the information rights field that also have an impact on the release of information and relating to information rights, and this chapter selects some of them for study .

16.2   Human Rights Act 1998

All elements of information rights legislation are based on this Act. It came into force in October 2000, at the same time as the Data Protection Act, and encompasses the 16 rights listed in the European Convention on Human Rights and its subsequent additions. Article 1 of the European Convention is an introduction, not included in the Act, and Article 13 is not part of the Act. The rights are:

- Article 2 Right to life
- Article 3 Prohibition of torture
- Article 4 Prohibition of slavery and forced labour
- Article 5 Right to liberty and security
- Article 6 Right to a fair trial
- Article 7 No punishment without law
- Article 8 Right of respect for private and family life
- Article 9 Freedom of thought, conscience and religion
- Article 10 Freedom of expression
- Article 11 Freedom of assembly and association
- Article 12 Right to marry
- Article 14 Prohibition of discrimination
- Article 1 of protocol 1 Protection of property
- Article 2 of protocol 1 Right to education
- Article 3 of protocol 1 Right to free elections
- Article 1 of protocol 13 Abolition of the death penalty.

The Act applies only to public authorities, and states that in all policies, actions and services provided the principles must be applied. Clearly, Article 8 has a major bearing on the Data Protection Act, including when accessing a deceased person's records, as this right extends after death. Article 10, freedom of expression, has a bearing on the exemption at section 36 of the Freedom of Information Act.

The Ministry of Justice is now promoting the use of this legislation and reminding public authorities of their duties to take it into account when making decisions.

16.3   Regulation of Investigatory Powers Act 2000

16.3.1 Overview

Article 8 of the European Convention on Human Rights is not an absolute right and can be qualified by a country's own laws. When the Human Rights Act came in it was realized that there was no law that permitted public authorities to carry out covert activity against an individual and, as a result, the Home Office introduced this legislation.

It is long, and in two parts, the first dealing with communications data and the second with surveillance data. It relates mainly to public authorities and places strict controls on how surveillance is to be carried out.

16.3.2 Communications data

This part makes it a criminal offence to intercept any form of communications, post, telephone (including mobile), internet (including e-mail) without consent or without the appropriate authority as laid down in the legislation. The content of any of these communications can only be accessed by the police or security services, and even then only on the specific authority of the Interception of Communications Commissioner (ICC). The remainder of the public sector covered by the Act can access only the details of calls made, including times and numbers, the subscriber's name if only the number is known, other subscriber information supplied to the phone company, titles of e-mails (but not the content). They cannot therefore open an unopened e-mail without consent, nor can they force a person to provide such consent. Remember that an e-mail of Charles.smith@blogwitch.gov.uk is sent to a personal e-mail address, so Charles should be asked whether someone else can access his e-mails in his absence or should use a generic, non personal e-mail address, e.g. information.rights@blogwitch.gov.uk for work-related matters.

If access is required to any of the other records mentioned above, certain conditions that should be observed:

- specific Home Office forms must to be completed
- authority needs to be given by a person listed on the Statutory Instrument 2003/3171

- it needs to be for one of the purposes named in the Act; for most authorities, including local authorities, the only purpose is for the detection and prevention of crime, so it must be a criminal offence that is being investigated
- the authority must have the power to carry out the investigations (i.e. the prosecuting authority, which is important in the case of a joint operation)
- applications must be processed by an authority's Single Point of Contact (SPoC).

An authority must have:

- trained authorizing officers at a level described in the statutory instrument
- a SPoC who has passed the appropriate examination and is accredited by the Home Office
- a Regulation of Investigatory Powers Act (RIPA) monitoring officer and
- a Senior Responsible Officer (SRO) who will have overall responsibility for overseeing RIPA. This person should be named and the name given to the Home Office.

Only the SPoC is permitted to contact the communications service providers to obtain information.

16.3.3 Surveillance

Part Two, dealing with surveillance, is very similar, except that a SPoC is not needed. There are three different types of surveillance, all of which are covert and all of which need the appropriate forms, regular reviews and renewals. Every case must be completed by a cancellation statement.

The three types of covert surveillance are:

- Intrusive – inside a domestic dwelling (including hotel rooms) or a private motor vehicle. This can only be carried out by the police or security services, and with the express consent of the Surveillance Commissioner

- Directed – against a specific individual or group of individuals
- Covert Human Intelligence Sources – where a person is placed to establish a personal relationship with the target in such a way that the target is not aware of what is happening.

Intrusive surveillance includes any covert activity inside a domestic premises where it is likely that personal information may be collected. This even includes information that is collected about, say, a trader, with the householder's consent. If it is about the trader's business activity, the information is not personal, but if there is a possibility of obtaining any personal information about the trader authority is required, remembering that this type of authority cannot be given other than to the police or security services.

Directed surveillance is the most common. There is a list of reasons permitting the police to use it, but most other public authorities can use it only for the detection or prevention of crime and disorder. It should be used only as a last resort and great care must be taken over collateral intrusion into another person's privacy.

Trading standards test purchases do not come under the Act as a personal relationship is not being created, only a business one. Similarly, noise tests are not monitoring what is being said in neighbouring premises, only the amount of noise in a particular place. In such cases the target is usually told by letter that noise levels will be monitored, which makes this investigation overt.

Covert Human Intelligence Source is more difficult to administer. This is a surveillance where an individual collects data about another by establishing a personal relationship, as opposed to a business one, with them and the subject is not aware that data about them is being collected. It is necessary to have a controller on call at all times when the source is operational and there is a requirement to carry out a risk assessment before engaging the source.

In all cases the Surveillance Commissioner and the Interception of

Communications Commissioner emphasize the requirement for the authorizing officer to review the proportionality of the surveillance in terms of the justifiability of intrusion into an individual's human rights.

16.3.4 Summary

While the methods of surveillance are encouraged by the two Commissioners, it is better to carry out surveillance in an overt manner, by putting up signs stating that an area is covered by CCTV, for example.

It is generally accepted that RIPA is paperwork heavy, but without these controls and monitoring the evidence collected can be declared unlawful and court cases have been known to collapse.

The basic test as to whether surveillance needs a RIPA authority is firstly, whether it is considered that the breach of an individual's human rights is justified and secondly, whether any member of the public would reasonably expect a breach of human rights in the circumstances. Therefore, using this test as well as the one stating that, in most cases, surveillance can only be carried out for detection and prevention of crime and disorder, surveillance for personnel issues it is not possible under the Act and, if carried out covertly, could be regarded as a breach of the Human Rights Act 1998. Surveillance where the individual is aware that it may be carried out is not regarded as covert.

Remember when administering any type of surveillance under either parts one or two the authorizing officer or designated person must ensure that all the tests have been applied properly, otherwise the surveillance may be unlawful.

16.4   Re-use of Public Sector Information Regulations 2005

These regulations (SI 2005/1515) came into force on 1 July 2005 and implemented the European Directive 2003/98/EC on the re-use of public sector information.

It was recognized by the European Parliament that the public sector holds a great deal of information that would be of commercial benefit to the private sector. The directive states:

One of the principal aims of the establishment of an internal market is the
creation of conditions conducive to the development of Community-wide
services. Public sector information is an important primary material for digital
content products and services and will become an even more important content
resource with the development of wireless content services. Broad cross-border
geographical coverage will also be essential in this context. Wider possibilities of
re-using public sector information should inter alia allow European companies to
exploit its potential and contribute to economic growth and job creation.

(Directive 2003/98 EC Recital 5)

As a result the directive was approved; it thus encourages the re-use of
information held by public sector bodies in each member state.

The purpose of the regulations is not to allow access to information – the
Freedom of Information Act and other access legislation does that – but to
provide a mechanism by which those seeking to re-use the information for
a purpose other than that for which it was produced can obtain permission
from those public bodies that control its use. One of the important
principles under the regulations is that re-use can only take place once
access has been granted. This includes material that has already been issued
or published by the public sector organization. In terms of previously
unpublished material, it could mean releasing material under Freedom of
Information legislation or other access legislation. The key point is that re-
use can only take place once the access hurdle has been cleared.

The supply of information in response to a Freedom of Information
request (or under any other access legislation) does not grant the recipient
an automatic right to re-use it. This is because the material is likely to be
covered by copyright, in most, if not all, cases pertaining to the public sector
information holder, and re-use such as publishing requires the copyright
owner's permission under UK law. This is explained in Office of Public
Sector Information (OPSI) guidance. Provision of information under the
Freedom of Information Act does not constitute a breach of copyright, but
its further use by the recipient, other than for private study, counts as re-use
for which permission is needed. In the UK this consent is often provided
through the issuing of a licence which can either be free or, in some cases,
subject to a fee.

It is recommended that responses to Freedom of Information requests include a statement explaining the position as follows:

> Most of the information that we provide in response to the Freedom of Information Act 2000/Environmental Information Regulations 2004 requests will be subject to copyright protection. In most cases the copyright will by owned by [insert name of public sector organization]. The copyright in other information may be owned by another person or organization, as indicated by the information itself.
>
> You are free to use any information supplied for your own use, including non commercial research purposes. The information may also be used for the purposes of news reporting. However, any other type of re-use, for example, by publishing the information or issuing copies to the public will require the permission of the copyright holder.
>
> For information where the copyright is owned by [insert name of public sector organization] details of the conditions on re-use can be found on our website at [insert details].
>
> For information where the copyright is owned by another person or organization, you must apply to the copyright owner to obtain their permission.
>
> (OPSI Guidance)

In terms of coverage of bodies, the scope of the Public Sector Information Regulations is somewhat narrower than for freedom of information. While the regulations, like the Freedom of Information Act 2000, cover central government and its agencies, local government, the health service, the Westminster Parliament, the Scottish Parliament and the Welsh Assembly, note that documents held by the following organizations are exempt:

- public sector broadcasters
- educational establishments (universities, colleges and schools)
- cultural authorities (museums, libraries, archives).

This list is not exhaustive and is only intended to give an indication of the scope.

Another key exemption is that of documents that public sector information holders produce outside their public task. The regulations, and the European Directive that the regulations implement, do not define 'public task' although OPSI's *Guide to the PSI Regulations* provides a useful explanation. To assess whether a public task is involved it is necessary to establish why a particular function is carried out and under what legislation. If an authority is using information gained under its normal functions for another use, that information should also be made available for re-use to other bodies. These other bodies should receive fair treatment and, for example, if a charge for re-use is being made it should apply also to the body's own re-use.

An applicant should make a request for re-use in writing. This application must include the name and address for correspondence, what documents are intended for re-use and how it is intended they will be re-used (regulation 6).

As mentioned earlier, re-use cannot take place unless access has already been cleared. This means that if information is exempt under freedom of information, for example, it is exempt from re-use. It is also exempt from re-use where the copyright is not owned by the public body. If to provide the information would require disproportionate effort, then the authority can provide a summary, create or adapt a document to comply with the request for re-use (regulation 11(3)) although there is a requirement to provide information by electronic means if at all possible (regulation 11(2)).

Charges for the right to re-use information should cover the costs of the information and a reasonable return on the investment (regulation 16). Under the regulations public sector information holders may charge the re-user a fee that covers the cost of collection, production, reproduction and dissemination of the documents, plus a return on investment. It should be noted that double charging is not permitted. For example, if a public sector organization has already charged the re-user for the cost of reproduction under a freedom of information request it cannot charge for this again under the PSI Regulations. The regulations require an authority to be transparent in the way it works. To do this it should publish the terms under which it will permit re-use and any charges that apply.

A public body has the same time limit of 20 working days as under the

Freedom of Information Act or Environmental Information Regulations, to respond to a request for a licence, although this can be extended, exceptionally, if a great number of documents is involved (regulation 8). The 20 day clock does not start until after the decision to allow access to the information has been made and so it does not run concurrently with an information rights request. If a decision whether or not to issue a licence has not been made by the twentieth day, the public body can notify the requester that this is the case, provided that they are also told when a decision will be reached (regulation 4(3)).

Public sector bodies, in common with any other copyright holder, can grant permission to re-use in a variety of ways. The permission to re-use is usually referred to as a copyright licence. There are many varieties of licence, ranging from a statement allowing users to download information from a website to a detailed contractual document. All licences have two things in common: they confer the right to copy copyright material and they generally contain some conditions of re-use. The conditions could include the payment of a fee, the need to acknowledge the copyright and the source, and an undertaking not to use the information in a misleading or detrimental manner. Significantly, OPSI has introduced a fast-track online licence known as the Click-Use Licence (there are several versions) and this provides a streamlined approach to the re-use of a wide range of material produced by central government and the Westminster Parliament.

Under the regulations there must be a consistent approach to the issue of licences and different organizations cannot be charged different sums for similar forms of re-use. Exclusive arrangements for re-use are allowed only if they are necessary for the provision of a public service and these should be made clear and published for public access. Under regulation 14 they need to be reviewed at least every three years.

Under the PSI Regulations public sector bodies are required to provide details of how to make a complaint through the body's internal complaints process. If the complainant is dissatisfied with how the complaint has been handled he may ask OPSI (the Office of Public Sector Information, part of The National Archives) to investigate the complaint. The complainant may also ask the Advisory Panel on Public Sector Information (APPSI) to investigate OPSI's findings if he remains dissatisfied. Both OPSI and APPSI publish their recommendations. The complaints process set out in the PSI Regulations does not preclude the complainant pursuing the matter through the courts at any stage of the process.

The regulations require public sector bodies to publish a list of documents that are available for re-use (regulation 16). This could be in the form of an information asset list. Each public body has an individual responsibility for putting in place its own scheme, but at central government level the Information Asset Register can be accessed centrally via Inforoute (www.uk-legislation.hmso.gov.uk/cgi-bin/searchIAR.pl?DB=iar).

OPSI has introduced the Information Fair Trader Scheme (IFTS) as a means of ensuring best practice in the area of information trading and re-use. It covers the principles of fairness and transparency. The IFTS was originally developed to cover major information traders within government such as Ordnance Survey and the Met Office. However, it has been extended to other public sector bodies. Full IFTS verification involves detailed audits carried out by OPSI. OPSI has also developed an online self-assessment version of the IFTS aimed at those public sector bodies that are not major information traders. The IFTS is essentially a process aiming to improve standards of information trading and re-use.

To summarize, a key theme of the regulations is that of transparency and fairness. They require that:

- individuals or bodies re-using public sector information in similar ways should be offered the same terms
- public bodies should be clear and transparent about the terms of re-use, including any charges
- applicants should know what information is available for re-use
- applications to re-use should be handled promptly, normally within 20 working days
- public sector bodies should have a complaints process in place.

In line with other information rights legislation, public bodies are encouraged to share best practice with others on the application of the regulations.

The Office of Public Sector Information issues some excellent free guidance on the subject which can be downloaded from its website at www.opsi.gov.uk/advice/psi-regulations/advice-and-guidance.

16.5   Summary

The three enactments, the Human Rights Act 1998, the Regulation of Investigatory Powers Act 2000 and the Re-use of Public Sector Information Regulations 2005, all relate in some way to access to information held in the public sector. All three are only applicable to public authorities and they should be used in conjunction with at least one of the main information rights trilogy.

The Office of Public Sector Information has provided not only the guidance referred to above but also sample licences which public sector bodies may consider using when implementing the legislation. The PSI Regulations provide authorities with an excellent means of controlling how information is used once it has been sent out – although it is not a money-making exercise.

How the legislation reviewed here and the main three information rights enactments interact will be examined in the next chapter.

17

Interaction of the legislation

17.1 Introduction

If you have read this book from the beginning, you will by now have a reasonable idea of how each of the three main enactments work. As has already been stated, none of them operates independently. The concept of a jigsaw in which each piece has its own identity but links with the others, so that only when they come together can the complete picture be seen, has already been mentioned. In this chapter you will see how each of the Acts needs reference to the others and how this is even written into the legislation and the codes of practice.

17.2 Access to personal data

Both the Freedom of Information Act and the Environmental Information Regulations refer to the Data Protection Act. They both make it clear at section 40 and regulation 13 that if the information falls under the definition of personal data as described under the Data Protection Act, then this is the legislation under which it should be handled. However, if the information is third party data, then, providing it relates to the public sector, the other two Acts may apply. Certainly information relating to deceased persons falls under the Freedom of Information Act but in this case reference to the Human Rights Act is necessary before it can be supplied. Reference to information about public sector officials is a very grey area insofar as an individual's expectation of privacy under the Data Protection and Human Rights Acts may be overridden by the public interest in releasing the data under freedom of information.

The Data Protection Act is the only legislation that overrides the Environmental Information Regulations when it comes to restrictions on releasing information.

17.3   Human rights

As was seen in Chapter 16, the Human Rights Act is the basis of all the legislation on information rights. The right of privacy is continued in the Data Protection Act and, for deceased persons, in the Freedom of Information Act. Without the Human Rights Act there would not have been the Regulation of Investigatory Powers Act, which also gives rights of access to personal information and overrules those sections of the Data Protection Act. The Human Rights Act also affects the Freedom of Information Act and the Environmental Information Regulations through its rights on freedom of expression, as this is the underlying element in those sections which allow authorities to remove data that would inhibit free and frank debate.

17.4   Environmental Information Regulations 2004

The regulations specifically mention both of the other enactments in the information rights trilogy. It has already been mentioned how the Data Protection Act is involved, but the regulations refer to the Freedom of Information Act so frequently that it becomes 'the Act' and refers to them directly, as they apply to the regulations as well.

17.5   Copyright and Re-use of Public Sector Information Regulations 2005

Release of information under freedom of information is not covered by the various copyright laws, although these should be mentioned in replies to requests, to show that copyright has not been waived and that the information should not be used without a licence, if this is appropriate. Sample phrases and full details are given in Chapter 16.4. This also emphasizes that the Re-use of Public Sector Information Regulations need to be complied with subsequent to the request requirements of the Freedom of Information Act.

17.6   Summary

It will be seen that there is often an overlap between each element of the various pieces of legislation. A request for information, when it comes in, can often refer to more than one Act or even all three. There is no requirement for a requester to mention under which legislation they want the information – that is up to the authority to determine, so they have to deal with a request under the Act that is most appropriate and, if necessary, the most favourable to the requester.

There are also other enactments that have a bearing on how a request is handled; some of these have been mentioned in earlier chapters. It can therefore be difficult if more than one team in an authority deals with requests.

It may be possible for the 'business as usual' requests to be handled in individual departments, but when it comes to data protection or the more complex requests, especially where exemptions are to be applied, then, unless they are handled in the same place, the task becomes almost impossible.

Some typical requests that could go across more than one piece of legislation are shown below.

'Why are you closing Highvale School, where will you be sending my Peter who is in year 6, and can I see his latest progress at school?' (Possibly freedom of information, data protection and education records.)

'Why did you move my father to Ward A where he contracted MRSA? How many other patients have contracted the infection in this ward and what happened to them? Have any staff contracted this infection, and if so, who?'

'What measures are being put in place to stop it happening again?' (Possibly freedom of information, environmental information regulations and data protection.)

It can be seen from these that it would be necessary to keep passing the request to at least three different teams if it were not handled at a central point. This would also affect the timeliness of any response and the consistency of the information released.

Having looked at the various aspects of information rights it is now time to bring together the basics of the legislation and summarize how to go forward.

18
Summary

18.1 Introduction

The various elements of information rights legislation have a big impact on the life of the individual and on those working in the public sector. Although the Data Protection Act also affects those outside the public sector there are certain parts that are unique to the public sector, especially those amended by the Freedom of Information Act.

The introduction of the various items of legislation means a culture change for any public sector authority. No longer is information just for their own use; it can also be shared, in the interests of greater understanding and accountability, with the public. Stories are frequently heard in the media where information has been obtained under the Freedom of Information Act; and the Data Protection Act is the one most frequently downloaded from the OPSI website. There is growing awareness (sometimes incorrect), of the legislation, some people thinking that everything an organization holds is available to them on request and that anything that might remotely mention them comes under data protection.

The appendices will remind you of the principles, the exemptions and exceptions, and list some useful documents to help authorities provide an effective and efficient service to the public. The rest of this chapter will highlight some of the most important points to be aware of.

18.2   Data Protection Act 1998

This is possibly the most complex piece of legislation on the statute books, and if there are a few key points to be remembered, they are:

- The eight data protection principles (Schedule 1 of the Data Protection Act and listed in Appendix 1 of this book) must always be applied to any work involving personal data.
- Organizations should make sure there are effective systems in place to handle requests for personal information and that all staff are aware of them.
- Organizations must always remember to tell the Information Commissioner if they are processing new data, or the same data for a different purpose.
- Individuals must be told if data is held about them, why it is being held and to whom it is being passed on.
- Personal information must be kept secure.
- Staff should be made aware of their obligations under the Act
- Checks should be made to ensure data can be handled lawfully.
- A named senior officer with responsibility for data protection is required in an organization.
- There needs to be a data protection champion at board level.

This Act affects everyone, both at work and at home, regardless of what they do. Data subjects are not just customers or service users but are also staff and contractors, and carelessness or error can cause considerable trouble.

18.3   Freedom of Information Act 2000

The objective of this legislation is to release information to the public, and this should always be at the forefront.

- The data should always be looked at with a view to releasing it rather than applying any of the exemptions.
- If exemptions are needed it is not usually the whole document that

will be exempt, but more usually only specific paragraphs or even words that will be taken out (redacted).

■   It is necessary to ensure the publication scheme is up to date and made available to staff as well as the public.
■   Staff should know how requests are to be handled and how to recognize them when they arrive.
■   There should be a senior named officer with responsibility for access to information.
■   There is a requirement for an information champion at board level.

This requires a culture change for many authorities and robust systems have to be in place for handling requests.

18.4   Environmental Information Regulations 2004

Many of the same points raised under freedom of information are applicable here but there are some additional ones to consider.

■   There are fewer exceptions under the regulations than there are exemptions under the Freedom of Information Act.
■   There is a duty to make new environmental information available electronically.
■   No other legislation, other than Data Protection Act, overrides the right to release of data under the regulations.
■   More organizations are covered by the regulations than by freedom of information.

Although the regulations are shorter than the other two enactments they are based on both European and international laws and agreements, so carry a great deal of weight.

18.5   Human Rights Act 1998

This is the basis for all the other legislation and therefore should always be considered. There is a statutory duty on public authorities to take this Act into consideration whenever considering any policy or procedure that they want to introduce.

18.6   Regulation of Investigatory Powers Act 2000

Authorities should make sure under this legislation that all the record-keeping procedures and authorizations are in place before proceeding with any surveillance or obtaining communications data. There are strict guidelines in place as to who can or cannot authorize data, shown in the table at Statutory Instrument 2003/3171, and what types of data can be accessed by which type of public authority. Make sure that all staff involved are trained and aware of their responsibilities. Authorities will need to appoint staff who can act as authorizing officer, senior responsible person, RIPA monitoring officer and, if necessary, Single Point of Contact.

18.7   Re-use of Public Sector Information Regulations 2005

These regulations are a newcomer to the information rights package but important nonetheless. While they are not compulsory they can be useful. If it is intended to introduce them in an authority, then an information audit needs to be prepared and kept up to date. Adequate methods of issuing licences also need to be in place. Remember that separate licences and fees for different types of requester are not permitted. Everyone must be treated equally, regardless of circumstances or purposes.

18.8   Records management

Records management is crucial to all aspects of information rights and should be introduced with care so as to make sure that records can be accessed effectively and efficiently. The following will be needed:

- an audit to find out what records are held
- standards on record titles and key phrases so as to aid quick retrieval
- measures to ensure records are kept secure
- a retention schedule, so it is known how long records should be kept

- the appointment of an officer, appropriately qualified, to oversee the operation of records management.

Without effective records management, requests for information will not be able to be handled properly; with such systems in place it is possible for substantial cost savings to be made. Remember The National Archives' comment, 'Records management can survive without information rights, but information rights cannot survive without records management'.

18.9 Training

Information rights is now becoming a recognized profession but not everyone needs to be up to the standard of a Master of Law. It is, however, important that all staff are aware of their obligations and duties under information rights legislation.

There are various ways in which this can be achieved, from specialist courses either in-house or pre-booked, such as those provided by information management trainers, to less formal awareness sessions for large groups of staff. These can be supported by online guidance or even an authority's policy statements.

The people involved in the day-to-day operation of the legislation should always keep on top of the latest decisions and interpretations by attending the appropriate conferences or using the Information Commissioner's and the Ministry of Justice's e-mail awareness facilities.

Evidence of training is always useful to have and some authorities are now instructing that a central list be kept of all staff attending information rights training. Training needs to be ongoing as the law develops, so authorities should develop a programme to ensure that new staff are informed of their duties as part of induction and that more experienced staff are kept up to date with new developments.

18.10 Summary

Information rights legislation can be as absorbing as you want to make it, it affects everyone whether they work in the public sector or not, and there is a growing awareness of the legislation on the part of requesters, the media and the public generally. Practitioners will be at the centre of their organization, dealing with a fascinating and growing area of work that is becoming even more important to the public sector as time goes on. This will provide a very challenging but extremely rewarding profession.

Appendix 1
Data protection principles

1 Personal Data shall be processed fairly and lawfully and, in particular, shall not be processed unless:
   (a) at least one of the conditions at Schedule 2 is met, and
   (b) in the case of sensitive data, at least one of the conditions at Schedule 3 is also met.
2 Personal data shall be obtained for one or more specified and lawful purposes, and shall not be further processed in a manner incompatible with that purpose or those purposes.
3 Personal data shall be adequate, relevant and not excessive in relation to the purpose or purposes for which they are provided.
4 Personal data shall be accurate and, where necessary, kept up to date.
5 Personal data processed for any purpose or purposes shall not be kept for longer than is necessary for that purpose or purposes.
6 Personal data shall be processed in accordance with the rights of the data subject.
7 Appropriate technical and organisational measures shall be taken against unauthorised or unlawful processing of personal data and against accidental loss or destruction, or damage to, personal data.
8 Personal data shall not be transferred to a country or territory outside the European Economic Area unless that country or territory ensures an adequate level of protection for the rights and freedoms of data subjects in relation to the processing of personal data.   (Data Protection Act 1998, Schedule 1)

Appendix 2
Flow chart of FOI

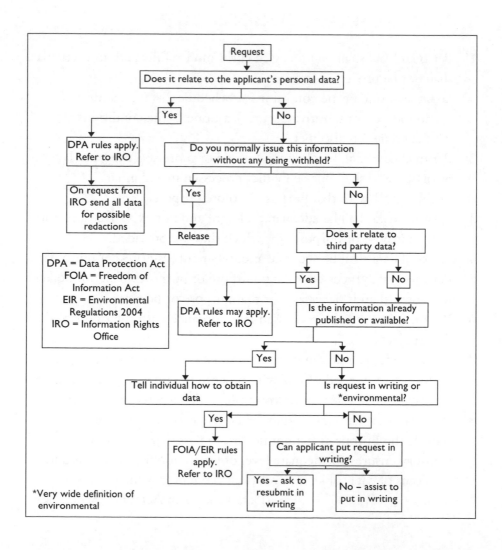

Request

Does it relate to the applicant's personal data?

Yes → DPA rules apply. Refer to IRO → On request from IRO send all data for possible redactions

No → Do you normally issue this information without any being withheld?

Yes → Release

No → Does it relate to third party data?

Yes → DPA rules may apply. Refer to IRO

No → Is the information already published or available?

Yes → Tell individual how to obtain data

No → Is request in writing or *environmental?

Yes → FOIA/EIR rules apply. Refer to IRO

No → Can applicant put request in writing?

Yes – ask to resubmit in writing

No – assist to put in writing

DPA = Data Protection Act
FOIA = Freedom of Information Act
EIR = Environmental Regulations 2004
IRO = Information Rights Office

*Very wide definition of environmental

Appendix 3
Exemptions and exceptions under the Freedom of Information Act 2000 and the Environmental Information Regulations 2004

Freedom of Information Act 2000

Section 21	Information accessible to applicant by other means.
Section 22	Information intended for future publication
Section 23	Information supplied by, or relating to, bodies dealing with security matters
Section 24	National security
Section 26	Defence
Section 27	International relations
Section 28	Relations within the United Kingdom
Section 29	The economy
Section 30	Investigations and proceedings conducted by public authorities
Section 31	Law enforcement
Section 32	Court records etc.
Section 33	Audit functions
Section 34	Parliamentary privilege
Section 35	Formulation of government policy etc.
Section 36	Prejudice to effective conduct of public affairs
Section 37	Communications with Her Majesty etc. and honours
Section 38	Health and safety
Section 39	Environmental information
Section 40	Personal information

Section 41   Information provided in confidence

Section 42   Legal professional privilege

Section 43   Commercial interest

Section 44   Prohibitions on disclosure

Section 14   Vexatious or repeated request

Section 12   Cost of compliance exceeds appropriate limit

Environmental Information Regulations 2004

Regulation 6   Information publicly available

Regulation 12(4)(a)   Not held

Regulation 12(4)(b)   Manifestly unreasonable

Regulation 12(4)(c)   Too general

Regulation 12(4)(d)   Unfinished material

Regulation 12(4)(e)   Internal communications

Regulation 12(5)(a)   International regulations, defence, national security or public safety

Regulation 12(5)(b)   Justice, fair trial, conduct an inquiry of a criminal or disciplinary nature

Regulation 12(5)(c)   Intellectual property rights

Regulation 12(5)(d)   Confidentiality

Regulation 12(5)(e)   Commercially confidential

Regulation 12(5)(f)   Interests of the person who provided information where (i) they were not under an obligation to supply or (ii) did not supply in accordance with any regulations or (iii) have not consented to disclosure

Regulation 12(5)(g)   Protection of the environment

Regulation 13   Personal data

Appendix 4
Bibliography and useful web addresses

Bibliography

Bichard Inquiry (2004) http://police.homeoffice.gov.uk/pdf/
   bichard-report.pdf.
Cape, E. (ed.) (2005) *RIPA 2000, Related SIs and Codes of Practice*,
   Thomson Sweet and Maxwell.
Carey, P. and Turle, M. (2006) *Freedom of Information Handbook*, Law
   Society.
Crocker, M. (2006) *Guidance on Records Management*, HMSO.
Michaels, P. (2004) *Accessing Environmental Information*, Local
   Government Association.
Pedley, P. (2003, 2006) *Essential Law for Information Professionals*, Facet
   Publishing.

Useful web addresses

Association of Chief Police Officers
   www.acpo.police.uk/asp/data/MoPI%20Guidance_INTER_
   03.03.06.pdf
Department for Constitutional Affairs
   www.dca.gov.uk or www.foi.gov.uk
Department for Environment, Food and Rural Affairs (DEFRA)
   (environmental data)

www.defra.gov.uk

Department of Health

www.dh.gov.uk/PublicationsAndStatistics/Publications/
PublicationsPolicyAndGuidanceN39

Email Preference Service

www.e-mps.org/en

JISC, Study of Records Lifecycle Structure: higher education
institutions,

www.jisc.ac.uk/indexcfm?name=srl_structure

Ministry of Defence

www.mod.gov.uk/publications/Freedom_of_Information_Act/rv/
rrsep05.htm

Ministry of Justice

www.justice.gov.uk

National Archives

www.nationalarchive.co.uk

www.nationalarchives.gov.uk/documents/managing_emails.pdf

www.nationalarchives.gov.uk/electronic_records/?source=ddmenu_
services2

www.nationalarchives.gov.uk/recordsmanagement/advice/pdf/
sch_disposal.pdf

National Association for Information Management

www.naim.uk.net

Office of the Information Commissioner

www.ico.gov.uk

Office of Public Sector Information

www.opsi.gov.uk/advice/psi-regulations/index.htm and

www.opsi.gov.uk (copies of legislation)

Records Management Society

www.rms-gb.org.uk

www.rms-gb.org.uk/resources/91

Statute Law

www.statutelaw.gov.uk

Appendix 5
Published standards for records management

British Standards

BS4783 – Storage, transportation and maintenance of media for use in
data processing and information storage
BS7799 – Code of practice on security management
BS DISC PD 0008 – Code of practice on legal admissibility and
evidential weight of information stored on electronic document
management systems
BS DISC PD 0010 – Principles of good practice for information
management
BS DISC PD 0012 – Guide to the practical implications of the Data
Protection Act 1998

International standards

ISO 15489-1 Information and Documentation – Records Management
Part 1 General

The National Archives

Various standards, www.nationalarchives.gov.uk/recordmanagement

Index